Let's Do Lunch

Love Defined by a Lifetime of Action

Hannah Rule

ISBN 979-8-89309-939-3 (Paperback)
ISBN 979-8-89309-940-9 (Digital)

Copyright © 2024 Hannah Rule
All rights reserved
First Edition

All rights reserved. No part of this publication may be reproduced, distributed, or transmitted in any form or by any means, including photocopying, recording, or other electronic or mechanical methods without the prior written permission of the publisher. For permission requests, solicit the publisher via the address below.

Covenant Books
11661 Hwy 707
Murrells Inlet, SC 29576
www.covenantbooks.com

For Rev. David August Paul, who taught us all how to give freely of ourselves, of our love, and of our lives

Contents

Foreword vii
Acknowledgments xi
Introduction: Why *Let's Do Lunch*? xv

Part 1: Love
Chapter 1:   What Is Love? 3
Chapter 2:   Sacrificial Love 10
Chapter 3:   Mutual Love 16
Chapter 4:   Equal Regard 20
Chapter 5:   Delivering Love 25

Part 2: In Action
Chapter 6:   Can We Embody Love? A Transformed Life 33
Chapter 7:   Will We Embody Love? A Choice Must be Made 38
Chapter 8:   Imitators of More than Love 42
Chapter 9:   You've Decided to Become Love, Now Have
             Some Fun! 49

Part 3: Changes Everything!
Chapter 10: The Gospel (Love Has Come) 57
Chapter 11: Applying Love 61
Chapter 12: A Changed World 67
Chapter 13: Love in Action Changes Everything 71

Epilogue: Why Tell David Paul's Story? He Gave Freely
of Himself, His Love, His Life 75

Foreword

In American sports, there is often a discussion of the "coaching tree," the collection of coaches who have been connected to or worked under a famous head coach. For example, Bill Belichick, a National Football League head coach for twenty-nine seasons, had seventeen assistant coaches under him go on to become head coaches in the NFL or college. Those head coaches had more than one hundred of their assistants go on to become head coaches. Truly, the long list of these coaches who can trace their professional calling back to Bill Belichick reads like a "Who's Who" of recent college and professional football head coaches.

In some Christian traditions, there may be some pastors who have such a "pastor tree" of former associates or church members who found their calling under the pastor's leadership. In Baptist life, especially nowadays, that's not as common as it perhaps once was. But, in all fairness, pastors like Rev. David A. Paul are not as common as they perhaps once were either.

Rev. David A. Paul was a minister, a juvenile court probation officer, a connector of people, a raiser of the downcast, a healer of the brokenhearted, and a friend to nearly everyone he met. To be clear, though, David wasn't just a do-gooder for those living on the wrong side of life's railroad tracks. David's sense of calling embodied the very best of Frederick Buechner's definition of *vocation*: "The place God calls you to is the place where your deep gladness and the world's deep hunger meet." For David—with an impish smirk, a raspy belly laugh, a caring touch, a listening ear, and an open hand—his deepest gladness was living, loving, and serving God and his neighbor. As someone who tragically lost his father at far too young an age, David also intimately knew the depths of anger, disillusionment, disappointment, and loneliness that come from life's searing challenges, especially for teenagers.

David would often talk privately about the challenges so many of his teenage probationers faced—broken homes, drug use, and abuse by the teens themselves, who were mostly modeling the example set by the adults in their lives, searching for love and acceptance from anyone who would notice them. David had seen his share of the shadow side of the teenage years, yet his deepest hopes for their redemption and restoration never wavered. I often wondered how David could continue to see the goodness in those teens when their lives and choices had clouded the rest of our perceptions of them. Surely, that was only possible because of David's deep and abiding faith in a God of second, third, and fourth (and even endless) chances.

That love of God, which fuels the never-ending possibility of redemption and restoration, also fuels the limitless capacity of the human spirit to serve others. For reasons that will never be known on this side of eternity, David Paul held tightly to that core Christian scripture and belief from James 2:26: "For just as the body without the spirit is dead, so faith without works is also dead." The grace of God offers us new life and a new way of being in this world and the next. The call to service, or "works," however, becomes a tangible and manifest way for Christians to respond to God's grace within the community and with their neighbor.

This entrenched sense of service as a response to God's love was the hallmark of David's ministry and the guiding north star of his life. Countless devotional thoughts, sermons, and conversations were offered by David to any who would hear—probationers, students, and church members alike. Serving others was not accidental; rather, the compulsion to sacrifice time, talent, and energy for the betterment of neighbors flowed from the boundless love of God, found most truly in the face and person of Jesus of Nazareth. To serve others takes intentionality and commitment to seeing someone else's life transformed. The following is a quote from Frederick Buechner.

LET'S DO LUNCH

> In the Christian sense, love is not primarily an emotion but an act of the will. When Jesus tells us to love our neighbors, he is not telling us to love them in the sense of responding to them with a cozy emotional feeling. You can as well produce a cozy emotional feeling as you can a cough or sneeze. On the contrary, he is telling us to love our neighbors in the sense of being willing to work for their well-being even if it means sacrificing our well-being to that end.[1]

Rev. David A. Paul's enduring and eternal faith in Jesus Christ as the savior of this world, and through whose love for us we, too, can know and experience love, shaped his life. That divine love's intrinsic call to service was the unifying force for David's teaching and pastoral ministry as well as his commitment to seeing the good in the face of strangers and friends alike.

To return to the coaching/pastoring tree analogy, by my estimation, David Paul had at least six of his former church youth ministry students go into Christian ministry or sense a call to ministry, including me. After graduating high school, my life was forever changed in the early summer of 1996 when, at Frenchie's Gas Station in south Bibb County, Georgia, David asked me to consider chaperoning a youth summer camp trip he was taking with his new youth group at another church. I did; and, as God's way leads on to way, I became the first ministerial associate to serve alongside David, serving for five years until I graduated college and went to seminary.

In my more than two decades of vocational ministry, I have seen more than ten students and ministry interns attend seminary following college graduation, further their education by studying religion in graduate school, or find their vocational calling in the service of the church. I have no doubt that my other friends who had David as their minister, pastor, and vocational guide have similar stories and

---

[1] Frederick Buechner, *Wishful Thinking: A Seeker's ABC* (Harper & Row, 1973), s.v. "Love," 53.

have had similar effects on others' vocational calling. David's life of loving service and his incalculable influence still reach far beyond anything I think he could have imagined.

William Sloane Coffin, venerable chaplain at Yale University and pastor at the Riverside Church in New York City, often offered the following benediction.

> May God give you the grace never to sell yourself short, grace to risk something big for something good, and grace to remember the world is now too dangerous for anything but the truth and too small for anything but love.

I think these words most clearly encapsulate the theology and spirit of David Paul. David believed in the unbridled potential in everyone, especially teenagers. He called so many to do something with their lives that mattered both for God and the world. He knew and believed that the truth would set you free, just as Jesus promised. He also knew that life was too short, too hard, and too complex for anything but love—especially love lived out in the service of others. May this be true for all of us too.

Rev. Jody Long, PhD

Acknowledgments

There are so many people who have prayed, supported, loved, and cared for me through this mustard seed of a dream given by God. I never dreamed of becoming a writer, and in fact, this dream only came a few years ago through God's prompts and nudging. This book was written during some of the hardest, most chaotic years of my life and was prompted by the deepest grief of my life—the loss of my father. Through the chaos, breakdowns, and exhaustion, I was lifted by so many who love me.

I want to first thank Patrick, my sweet husband. You have supported me through so many changes, challenges, disappointments, joys, mountaintops, and valleys. You did not sign up to marry a woman perpetually in grad school with no full-time job for the first five years of marriage, but you have always been there with a hug and ice cream in hand. You helped me make wise, logical decisions when I would usually just jump headfirst, hoping not to fall. You encouraged me when I felt lost and made sure to send tons of puppy videos to make me smile. I truly would not be where I am without you.

I want to thank my mother, Beth, for teaching me to always go and do. You have guided me through so many seasons of life, and you have done it all with grace. You are one of my favorites to laugh at inside jokes with ("Jesus will be with us to the very end of the edge"), talk things through with, and adventure with. I know this was a book about what Dad taught us, but he could not have followed God's call as well without you. You didn't marry a minister, but God sure did know the perfect wife for Rev. David Paul.

I want to thank Brian Everett and his sweet family. Brian has been an integral part of my life since before I was even born. He watched me grow up, went to my high school and college graduations, officiated at my wedding, and preached at my ordination. Brian was the first person I sent *Let's Do Lunch* to before I ever knew there would be a part especially about him. I know that my father's legacy will not only last in memories of him but in the legacy that Brian has left.

I want to thank my brother, Darryl, for being my go-to for advice and much of the technical side of this process. You have always had my back, from when we were little to adulthood. You have encouraged and supported me through the many career changes and new paths. And you gave me two of my favorite titles: Aunt Hannah to sweet Felicity and sister-in-law to the best, Brenda.

I want to thank Tom, Pam, Caleb, and Chelsea Rule. I have won the jackpot of in-laws. I never dreamed of feeling like I belonged to two families, but you have done just that. You all have encouraged me, guided me through difficult decisions, and supported me through my many changing paths. And I get to be Aunt Hannah to two of the best, Elijah and Ella.

I want to thank my childhood best friend, Haley Phillips. You have seen it all. You knew me as an awkward preteen, a nerdy college student, and a chaotic adult. You sat and cried with me through some of the toughest seasons I have ever had. And I had the honor to cry with you through some of yours. God knew what He was doing when He connected us way back in the fourth grade at church. You have always been a great strength in my life and have continually guided me to hope in Jesus.

I want to thank my sweet friends Amy Goldin, Melissa Roth, and Kristen Vick. You have been some of my most steadfast friends for over fifteen years. We may not get to see one another often, but I know you are just a text or phone call away. I cannot possibly explain how every Milledgeville trip, call, text, message, and meal has meant to me. You have always been such an encouragement and support for me as I have navigated the chaos of the last decade.

I want to thank Casey Wayne for encouraging and guiding me throughout this writing journey and for years before. I also want to thank Emily Woods, Leah Williams, and Ali Duckworth for being such amazing supporters and friends through some of the highest highs and lowest lows.

I want to thank our New City Church Missional Community. You all have been such a support that we desperately needed during a chaotic season. I have cherished each of your prayers and friendships.

I want to thank Bonni Berkowitz, Sandra Jarvis, and the team from Covenant Books. You walked out on a limb for a book I never thought would be published. Thank you for making this process as smooth as possible.

Introduction

Why *Let's Do Lunch*?

> Little children, let us not love in word or
> talk but in deed and in truth.
> —1 John 3:18

Love seems like one of the simplest subjects. We feel it. We say it. We want it. We need it. But do we want to *be* love? Can love be the theme or even the entire point of our lives? Love seems easy until it is applied as a life action. We talk about love so much but do little to explain how to make it part of our lives. There are plenty of books out there, right? Does the world need yet another book explaining how we should live? Probably not. Then why write *Let's Do Lunch*? I have heard from other authors that many decide to write because they haven't found what they want to be reading. Cue motivation number one.

I have seen so many books out there explaining the correct way to live. Some of these are biblical, and some are not. Some are even great self-help books that have helped millions live happy lives. But how many of these books show you how to love? Very few of these books explain just how to do it. I cannot tell you how many times I have heavily agreed, head nodding so hard it triggered my vertigo, with how some have said we should live. I finish these books so excited to go out and live such an amazing, purpose-filled life but then realize the steps to do this were not explained, and there is no why to the purpose. Now this is not absolute. There are some authors and leaders I have read or followed that have indeed given biblical advice on how to live and then the steps on how to live and love like Jesus. They are the second motivation for this book.

Authors like Dr. David Gushee and Bob Goff have given me definitions and actions to living out love in everyday life. Through learning from them and reading their books, I have come to the conclusion that we as people struggle to understand how to actually love. We struggle to understand what love really is, and how it can be shown. We also struggle to understand how to live a life that is truly grounded in true love because we refuse to let our actions be led in love. It is really easy to say that we love others, but it is another idea to truly live out those words. Our motivations rarely match the motivations of someone becoming Love.

The authors above did not miss the mark by any means, but I think we need more examples of how we actually imitate Jesus in becoming Love. I have read through the stories of the Bible, especially the stories we are taught show us how to apply God's commands. But the funny thing is, it can be hard to visualize this type of obedience within our context. I'm not saying that it is impossible to understand the application of loving like Jesus because of a change in cultural context. It may just be difficult to know how to live it out, which decreases our motivations for even trying. I am way less likely to step out in faith in becoming Love if I am unsure of how to do it. Who can I look to for this example? My father.

I have been a witness to someone embodying the love, grace, and kindness of Jesus in a way that did not just tell people how to live but presented this truth with their very life. The person I have in mind happens to be my father, Reverend David August Paul. As he loved so many people, he will be referred to by many different names: Dave, Reverend, Mr. Paul, David, DAP, Dad, dear, and sir. He was a reverend, a best friend, a coworker, a father, a husband, a son, a brother, a counselor, a father figure, a pastor, and a probation officer. But my father's true identity was becoming Love with every step, every word, and every person he met, becoming an invitation to live life through the action of love.

Many who know me knew him well, but they may not know that he was also an author. That's right, he started writing a book. He was compelled to write down thoughts and ideas about the woman I was becoming. I still have not fully processed what that means to me. Reading about your own life in the words of someone else is a great way to do some soul searching. I have read his words over and over, hoping that I am or am becoming the woman he thought of. The woman he hoped I would be. As a woman in my thirties still figuring out life, what did he see that he thought needed to be written down? Is my life really worth remembering as a written work of my father's passion?

My father thought so, and that was the man that he was for every person he met. He listened to them and really saw them for who they were even if they did not know yet. He only finished the introduction before he passed away, but I guess we should label that motivation number three. I now get to finish the task he started. I get to show the world, or maybe just my laptop, just what love looks like. At times he may seem too good to be true while other times his missteps may bring the feeling of embarrassment, but weaved all throughout this story will be love. Love was the theme of his life because it was lived through his actions.

Are you ready? Buckle up. It's going to be a bumpy ride.

PART 1
LOVE

Chapter 1

What Is Love?

> Love is something you do, not merely something you say.
> —Tony Evans

In our world, love can mean many different things. I super-duper love Oreos. I believe they may have been the first cookie I ever had, and I want it to be my last at the end of my time here on earth. I believe God has an Oreo station just for me in heaven. They really are just that good.

I deeply love my mother. We can talk for hours and not get tired. The interesting part about love is that it can look different even with the same person. When I was a teenager, I definitely loved my mother, but I didn't really want to spend hours talking with her (teenage angst, am I right?). We now can shut down restaurants after sitting and talking for so long.

If I can describe love for Oreos and love for my mom with the same word, it must mean that they are the same! But they are not the same. Confused yet? Maybe love is more complicated than we first thought. How can I say that I love Oreos and my mom and others without defining what that love really means? Can something that sounds so simple actually be super complex? Maybe! Let's find out.

Loving everybody always, as Bob Goff says, can seem super overwhelming. It can seem overwhelming because it is commanded by Jesus, who is the definition of love. When we are trying to love like Jesus, we can feel inadequate because we can never fully love perfectly. Even in the small amount of information we have of Jesus's ministry, it can be seen that love is the theme. He sits with people, asks about them, pays attention to those everyone else ignores, and seeks to draw people closer rather than alienating. That list is intimidating! If this is what real love looks like, how in the world are we supposed to do it?

"For Christians, love is the heart of living, of being human. Love is at the heart of the life of Christ, his teaching, and his death on the cross" (David Gushee, *Kingdom Ethics*, p. 107).

Another one of my favorite authors is C. S. Lewis, and he wrote about four definitions of love: affection, friendship, eros, and charity. We understand love to be in these categories, and God has used these categories so that we might be able to imitate divine love. These definitions help explain the many layers of God's divine love, which is the love the Father gave Jesus that Jesus then gave the world that the world has been trying to imitate. In order to understand how we become Love, we should understand how Jesus became Love.

C. S. Lewis described two major ideologies around love as gift-love, which is the "love which moves man to work and plan and save for the future well-being of his family," (C. S. Lewis, *The Four Loves*, p. 1) and need-love "that sends a lonely or frightened child to its mother's arms." Gift-love and need-love are what many humans think to be what love truly is, work toward taking care of others or basic neediness. Though that leaves out how God works through love. Divine love is gift-love because "the Father gives all He is and has to the Son. The Son gives Himself back to the Father, and gives Himself to the world and for the world to the Father, and thus gives the world (in Himself) back to the Father, too." We know (*divine*) love not because of feelings, but because of *Jesus*.

"By this we know love, that he laid down his life for us, and we ought to lay down our lives for the brothers" (1 John 3:16).

"And this is love, that we walk according to his commandments; this is the commandment, just as you have heard from the beginning, so that you should walk in it" (2 John 6).

Need-love is then established as our born helplessness because "we need others physically, emotionally, intellectually; we need them if we are to know anything, even ourselves." When God loves humanity, it is divine gift-love; God does not wait for our love in return but instead gives humanity Jesus for us to understand that Love now has a name, Jesus. When humanity loves God, it is need-love because humanity was created to need God and others. Humanity cannot love God as divine gift-love because we need that love back, but God can have divine gift-love because, while we need God's love, God does not need ours.

We cannot fully embody divine love (*gift-love*) because of our inherent *need-love*, but we can imitate it.

Now that we have established that love may be more complex than we have realized, we will learn some definitions of love through the chapters of this book. We will look out for four main definitions: sacrificial love, mutual love, equal regard, and delivering love. I learned these definitions in my Ethics course at McAfee School of Theology taught by Dr. David Gushee. We learned these definitions in his book, *Kingdom Ethics: Following Jesus in Contemporary Context*. When we went over these definitions, I immediately thought about my father and how he lived his life. Through these definitions and the actions of my father, I have learned that love is not only a feeling or even actions. Just as I stated above, love is a person, and love has a name, and that name is Jesus. Is it possible to embody all four of these definitions? Why are these definitions important to living a life ruled by love?

Through the definitions, love can be seen as sacrifice, communion, service, compassion, and the combination of all. It is rare for a person that is not Jesus to be able to embody and live out the wholeness of love. Human instinct is not to love but to be selfish. In our simplest forms, humans will look out for themselves and protect themselves over others. Understanding the importance of love will help us step outside of our human character in order to move love from a spoken word into a daily action.

Love is important because it is why we exist. If God is love, and Jesus is the true embodiment of love, then our existence is to glorify that love and reflect it onto others. The moment we decide to follow the path of Jesus, we are called to walk in love. We are called to sacrifice, have compassion, listen to people that may hate us, and help people that we feel do not deserve our help. It is not a choice; it is a daily calling upon our lives. Living a life ruled by love means taking all of these definitions into account. If we want to embody love, we cannot love with only equal regard but not love sacrificially or mutually. They work together in order to reflect Jesus as much as humanly possible. While I have said I love Oreos, love is more complex and has many layers that can be reached for every single day.

One of the most quoted scripture passages about love would be in Luke 10:27: "And he answered, 'You shall love the Lord your God with all your heart and with all your soul and with all your strength and with all your mind, and your neighbor as yourself.'"

The catch to this realization of how to love is questioned by the man asking Jesus "who is my neighbor?" The idea of loving others like we love ourselves seems to be pretty easy, but Jesus responded with the parable of the Good Samaritan, which results in the merciful hero of the story being the enemies and second-class citizens, the Samaritans. This is the first challenge in imitating divine love to work to become Love: loving difficult people that may hate you. We will discuss more about how we go about loving difficult people in a later chapter.

Another aspect of the passage from Luke would be that we are to love our neighbors as we love ourselves. This statement assumes you love yourself a great deal, but what if you do not? One of my favorite authors, Annie F. Downs, wrote: "How we love ourselves informs how we love others" (*Chase the Fun*, p. 167). If we are struggling to love others, we may need to take a look at how we love ourselves. Are we picking out every flaw we see in ourselves? Are we belittling our achievements? Are we convincing ourselves that God has not possibly called us to the path we are on? As we begin to dissect how we may not be loving others well, we may come to find that we are also not loving ourselves well. Being imitators of divine love means that we understand that we all receive the gift-love from God and that we should work to imitate this truth.

LET'S DO LUNCH

One way I have been reminded to love myself well how Jesus loves me is encouragement through my friend, Courtney Reimer. Our friendship started on a random adventure trip to Uganda with Bob Goff's organization, Love Does. I joined about fifteen strangers from all over North America to adventure with Love Does, joining their organization in the beautiful work they are doing in Uganda. From the moment I met Courtney, I could tell we would be friends. She shined joy from her whole being, her kindness flowed around from person to person being led by her joyful smile and inclusive presence. As we became friends, Courtney also became close to Scott Reimer (peep that last name!). Scott and Courtney would begin their beautiful relationship right there in Uganda, but only after Scott asked her a question no potential boyfriend ever asked: "How is your relationship with God?" Courtney later explained to me that this was the most unexpected question because she did not really have a relationship with God. From that day forward, God has been bursting through Courtney as she lets Him guide her through His steadfast love and provision. Courtney and Scott would later get married, Courtney leaving Texas to be married to Scott in Canada, and God would continue to use their relationship to blow us all away by showing others God's love. One amazing miracle that came from this relationship: She Wears Worth.

She Wears Worth is an organization created by Courtney to help encourage girls and teens that they are worthy and that their worth comes from their loving Creator. Courtney organized clothing drives, the Never Unnoticed Clothing Pop-Up event, and now a She Wears Worth Conference for teenage girls in the Winnipeg, Canada, area. Courtney began to shine not only joy and happiness but also the love of Jesus through her desire for girls and teens to know their worth. If you have never been a teenage girl, I will let you know it is a tough place to be. Body types become impossible trends to keep up with. The pressure to have a boyfriend and to be liked weigh heavy, and the understanding of self-worth is murky at best. Courtney grew up chasing worldly beauty standards and was never satisfied and wanted to change this struggle for the girls around her. She Wears Worth has launched merchandise, a podcast, a conference, and pop-up events all created to show girls they are worthy to be loved by their Creator and by themselves. Courtney has not only encouraged the teens to feel their worth but also encouraged me, a grown woman in her thirties that has always struggled to love herself. While I was very blessed to understand this definition of love through my upbringing, I have struggled with knowing my work separate from my production, how much I have helped others, and by the standards of those around me.

My parents were intentional about showing their love to my brother and I, and they reminded us to actively love and be kind to others. A quote that I recently found states: "You are an image-bearer with work to do, not a work-doer with an image to maintain."

My parents taught us to listen to other perspectives first before judging not because my parents are saints and righteous people, but because they were doing their best to be image-bearers of Christ and teaching us to do the same. We have been confronted with racism about others in the community, judgment about those without an address, and condemnation for others labeled as "sinners." In each situation, my parents responded in love as image-bearers and not just people maintaining this Christian image. We were told to be kind, listen to the perspective of others, and always give the benefit of the doubt. I can still remember multiple instances when my mother heard about an injustice and said to a friend of mine that she looked up the establishment and reported the worker that spouted the racist language.

We were taught this type of love and respect of others at an early stage that I did not understand why my classmate was being so rude to my friend in second grade. I remember the disgust coming from this classmate that I would dare share my jacket with my African American friend when we sat together on the dirty floor of our classroom trailer. It never occurred to me that my friend's race did anything other than being a beautiful part of her amazing identity. It never occurred to me to think of her simply as her race then as a whole person. Being raised in a home that looked to find the good in others even when it seemed impossible was a home that was becoming Love.

Love may seem more complicated based on these definitions and examples, but I never questioned acts of love as a child. My parents worked hard to become Love so that I could see a world where love changes everything. Later in life, I would find out that not everyone had this experience. Not everyone had a father who would listen before judgment or creating a solution or punishment. Not everyone would have a mother that would teach her children that even the kids in school that made fun of her were to still be treated respectfully. Not everyone had a mother that would stoke the curiosity of learning about others rather than judging people's first impressions. Being raised in a home where the action of Love was seen daily made my journey of becoming Love less complicated because I had people to watch that modeled for me.

But how did my parents know to live their lives like this? They learned what becoming Love looked like by looking at Jesus.

Chapter 2

Sacrificial Love

> Taking a bullet for someone you love is impressive, but taking a grenade for those that hate you, that is love.
> —Anonymous

Anders Nygren was a Swedish bishop that published *Agape and Eros* in 1932 and defined agape love as sacrificial love. "Such love is purely unselfish, spontaneous, and unmotivated by any value of benefit the other might have for us. It is not created by any value it sees in others but instead creates value in them" (*Kingdom Ethics*, p. 108). Sacrificial love gives value to the receiver of the love rather than the giver. Most of our positive emotions and actions give value to the person showing the positive action or emotion. If you are giving, others look at you as a good person. If you are kind, others find that characteristic of value in you. Sacrificial love is not about the one that shows it but that the one that shows it values the receiver so much that they would give without hesitation. That is what makes this type of love so rare. It is extremely difficult to do an entirely selfless act without the motivation to look good or to show your positive characteristics.

You may be thinking, *Wow! What a way to start off this book. This is an impossible task!* While sacrificial love was demonstrated perfectly through Christ, we are called to be imitators of Christ and should strive to become Love. "The pitfalls of sacrificial love are not small. Sacrificial love can be used to perpetuate oppression, can create martyrs, it can be impossible to reproduce, and can neglect self-concern" (*Kingdom Ethics*, pp. 109–110). I was fortunate enough to have a man as a father that modeled this in the best ways I have ever seen and did not use sacrificial love to lift himself higher or harm others. Though my father loved others' well-being, great model of sacrificial love, he was not perfect.

If you have never been to Macon, Georgia, you may not understand all of my references. Macon is my home. It is where I grew up, where I made friends, where I found my personal faith, and where my father based his ministry. He also grew up in Macon, and some that are from Macon may not think a lifetime here is a goal that anyone has. There are rough areas just like any major city would have. My dad tended to see these areas not as places to run and hide from, but places to go and love. During his time as a juvenile probation officer and a youth pastor, he went all over middle Georgia caring for teenagers.

During a youth outing with his second youth group as a youth pastor, he took his group to grab some food late after a youth event. They ended up at Burger King (lots of cheap fast food is a staple for teenagers). It was during this trip that outside of the restaurant, one of the youths got into an argument with a stranger. Dad intervened and ended up briefly standing in between his youth and a stranger with a gun. Now nothing happened that night. No one was hurt. There was no fight, and everyone went home just fine, but that is not the only way that night could have ended.

There was no question in Dad's mind as to what he was doing. I was a small child when this occurred, and I was not told of this until I was in my twenties after his death. Looking back, I can see, as his daughter, I would have hoped he would have thought about us and to not place himself in danger, but knowing his call to love, I know exactly why he did it. His youth was just a kid and needed someone to advocate for him. The definition of *advocate* according to Google is "a person who publicly supports or recommends a particular cause of policy." Dad stood between a teenager making a poor decision and a gun not because the teenager was right, but because that teenager deserved to have another chance at life. I do not know what would have happened if Dad had not stepped in, but I know Dad would have never willingly let something happen to any of his youths. God's love works similarly to this but in the most perfect, excellent way. We were given the perfect advocate for us all through Jesus.

God so desperately wants to be in a relationship with us. We get the choice as to who or what we worship and love. That is a human characteristic given in the image of God. When we choose over and over to step away from God, God helps make a way back. Not because God wants to control but because, as we are created beings, we are most whole with our Creator. Throughout history, humans continue to think they will be whole with many different things. Over and over we place creatures and other created things higher in our lives as things that will make us whole. But wait! What makes us think that something created in this world will make us whole more than our Creator? History reveals no one apart from God can claim full wholeness. So God made a way: love, and love has a name, Jesus.

Sacrifice sounds like a scary word especially when we place the word alongside Jesus. Jesus, God in flesh, became human, lived a life of a servant ministering to others. He then willingly gave his life in place for us. Sacrifice sounds pretty scary. It sounds like you will lose everything, and losing everything can become a legitimate fear. We all spend our lives accumulating enough "stuff," whether that stuff is wealth, possessions, people, or success. Maybe thinking that sacrifice means giving up something is too much of a surface idea. How about we go deeper?

When we think of the word *sacrifice*, we think of what we value or what we hold the closest. This can be something different for each and every person. What we value is what we invest in. We can invest our money, time, effort, health, and even our lives. What would you sacrifice to keep your family safe? I had the honor of watching my father live a life of sacrifice. He gave him money, time, and was willing to give his life not only for us, his family, but also for all others.

Love that is sacrificial is also contagious. My father's best friend was Brian Everett. Dad had been Brian's youth pastor in my dad's first youth group. Brian and Dad were only eleven years apart, so when Brian grew up, they grew their friendship as adults in the ministry. Brian followed suit and became a chaperone for Dad's youth trips. Brian pursued counseling as a career but was always involved in ministry at least part time. He would go on to have his own youth group and would have his youths join my dad's youth group on trips and retreats. They had the best time showing teenagers the love of Jesus. Brian always had the best words remembering my dad after he passed. Below is a social media post by Brian on the fifth-year anniversary of my father's death:

> Five years ago today, my wingman, David Paul, broke formation with direct orders to return to Home Base. He flew into the portals of heaven and into the arms of our Lord. David always responded when the Master called. He did the same when called into ministry…he responded with everything he had. David sacrificed his desires, his money, his health, and, even at times, family and friends to pursue after what God told him to do; sharing Jesus with teenagers until his last breath. I miss him on this journey through life, but rejoice in his legacy and our Blessed Hope. Until then… (Everett)

My father sacrificed whatever God asked in order to love people well. I included this story about Brian because as I write this, Brian was called to return to "Home Base" as he put it, less than two weeks ago, September 9, 2021. This is how I know my father was becoming Love and loving others through action, Brian Everett. Dad made such an impact on Brian's life that Brian could not help but love others through his actions as well. We are still currently in a global pandemic, but Brian's funeral was packed, and the live streamed service was overwhelmed with the amount of people that were touched by his life. That's the most interesting part about becoming Love, others want to join. Brian became a safe haven for those of us that lost my father. He loved us, mentored us, officiated many weddings my dad would have officiated, wrote countless recommendation letters, and took care of us the way my dad would have. I even gave him the beginning pages of this book to read. I never got his thoughts on it, but he did recommend I be sure to finish it. Love that is sacrificial is also contagious.

As we try to live a life of sacrifice in order to love people fully, we can often do this in the wrong way. We can lay down everything for others, which can in turn harm ourselves. This leads me to a story about my dad that was not one of his best moments. My dad was a person that would be there for anyone if they needed him. He would even sacrifice time with us, his family, and ignore others to be there for others. One instance was my father running to the hospital bedside of a youth on Mother's Day. While Mother's Day is not the most important day for my mother and my family, it is a day we can set aside to celebrate our family together. The youth ended up being okay and had support. My dad was there for many hours. I go back and forth with this because I can see myself doing it. I can absolutely see myself sit with a family in the hospital because they needed support. While my family and my mother were not really mad at my dad for going to the hospital, it was another day not spent together as a family. He often wore himself out being there for others, being everything for everyone, and that often left little of himself for our family. I do not regret having such a loving man as a father, but I can see how that level of sacrifice is not sustainable.

Before he died, my mother remembers him watching some television show and jumping up in order to jot down a quote he had just heard. That quote was "Give freely, of yourself, of your love, of your life" (Anonymous). I was told about this quote after he passed. We decided that quote should be on his grave marker because he did exactly that. He gave himself, which included his health, wealth, time, and energy, to loving others. He gave his love not only by being charitable but also by walking alongside people in their hurt. He gave his life, which included his very breath. My dad was not inhuman or a genius; he was just a follower of Christ. He did not come up with this way of life on his own. He took Jesus's call to lay down his life and follow Him seriously. This command from Jesus in the Gospel of Matthew says it best:

> Then Jesus told his disciples, "If anyone would come after me, let him deny himself and take up his cross and follow me. For whoever would save his life will lose it, but whoever loses his life for my sake will find it. For what will it profit a man if he gains the whole world and forfeits his soul? Or what shall a man give in return for his soul?" (Matthew 16:24–26)

My father denied himself. He denied his selfishness (most of the time), his pride (most of the time), and his greed. He lived every single day knowing that he was put on this earth to show people they are loved and that they matter. That was his cross. His burden to bear. Throughout his life, my father would give up his money, time, and put his reputation on the line to reach out to others in love. This was not a light cross or burden to bear. He was often misunderstood by people on the outside looking in. Many did not fully understand why he would stand in front of a gun for a teenager that lived for making life difficult for others. Many did not fully understand why he would give his hard-earned cash to those experiencing homelessness. As Bob Goff says, "Loving people the way Jesus did means living your life being constantly misunderstood."

Chapter 3

Mutual Love

> For I long to see you, that I may impart to you some spiritual gift to strengthen you—that is, that we may be mutually encouraged by each other's faith, both yours and mine.
> —Romans 1:11–12

Daniel Day Williams wrote the book *The Spirit and the Forms of Love*, and Williams argues that the sacrificial agape love that Nygren speaks of does not fully contain the love of Christ. Williams discusses that "God deeply desires our response of love. God wants love to be mutual love. Love is not a one-way street running from God to us, in which God has no motive, does not seek any return of love from us, and is unaffected by our love or unfaithfulness. Rather, God wants mutual love, personal communion in which we give love back to God" (*Kingdom Ethics*, pp. 110–111).

This does not belittle what we have learned about sacrificial love because for Christ to have perfectly loved all of creation and given his life for the sake of being close to creation is absolutely the character of God. Sacrificial love also does not require reciprocated love, but God loves to be in communion with creation. Mutual love creates an interpersonal relationship between God and Creation.

One of the most difficult parts of ministry is getting people to understand you are not superior and understanding, that if you minister and serve others, that does not make you better than them. My own experience with ministry work spans a few different environments: youth ministry, children's ministry, foster care worker, homelessness ministry, hospital chaplaincy, and nursing home ministry. Throughout time, many can see these positions and experiences as authoritative or maybe even "more Christian" than others. This is the exact opposite of what most, if not all, ministers strive to do. In this example, love is not just merely sacrificial. It must also be mutual.

Mutual love is reciprocal love, which highlights interpersonal communion. We may strive to love others as Christ loves, which can give a major focus on sacrificial love. We can then forget that Christ demonstrated mutual love to many he interacted with. Jesus would pull up a seat and share a meal with just about anyone. One of my favorite stories of Jesus showing mutual love was with Zacchaeus.

For those that do not know the story of Zacchaeus, he was a tax collector living in Jerusalem during the time of Jesus. He was not only a tax collector (many people did not trust tax collectors and thought they were all thieves) but also the very example of what people were afraid of. He made money off of overcharging people and keeping their money for himself. He had gained massive wealth by taking from others. When Jesus came to town, he attracted a lot of crowds. Think your favorite sports star, musician, and actor all rolled into one. Zacchaeus heard Jesus was in town and wanted to see what all the fuss was about, but there was one problem. Zacchaeus was shorter than the rest of the crowd and could not see. So he climbed a tree to get a glimpse. When he did this, Jesus spotted him, knew who he was, and immediately asked to come over and eat at Zacchaeus's home.

Why would Jesus, the miracle worker, and Savior to the world ever be caught at a tax collector's home, especially a tax collector like Zacchaeus? Because Jesus loves through communion. Jesus knew that loving people started with being with them face to face. Sitting with them on even ground. Jesus may have become very famous and always drew a crowd, but he never let how people regarded him to change how he treated others. Eating with Zacchaeus was not about Jesus performing love in front of the crowd. It was about getting face to face with Zacchaeus and forming a relationship with him.

Mutual love is another aspect of love that can seem so hard for us to do. Many times, we do good things for others partially because they need help and partially because it makes us feel good. We feel good about ourselves when we love others and especially when we are seen loving others. What if we embodied mutual love by remembering that we are indeed no better than others and need to be loved just as much? What would the world look like if love was all even and not on a scale of who deserves the most?

My father lived a life of mutual love better than most people I have seen. While he was not a licensed counselor, he did learn how to listen to others well and would ask the best questions in order for someone to feel loved and love themselves more. His response to someone needing to talk or needing guidance was "Let's do lunch!" He knew that the best environment for this type of relationship and connection was to be comfortable over food and on even ground. He put himself in a position of equality with anyone that sought his help. I was even lucky enough to hear "Let's do lunch" a few times as an adult. Those words were not just his way of making a plan. He used those words to indicate that they were worth his time, and they deserved a safe space to talk and have someone genuinely listen.

We often only offer this kind of love to those that are like us. This is usually people we are comfortable around, people that understand who we are, and whom we can easily make conversations with. The interesting thing about mutual love is that it is for everyone. That meal at Zacchaeus's house was probably a bit uncomfortable. He was known as a hustler and a thief to everyone in town. In today's time, it is usually the outward appearance that we first judge. A teenager with slouching clothing, a woman wearing old, worn-out clothes we would label lazy. We even look at ethnicity or culture to measure what kind of person we are interacting with even if we do not consciously mean to jump to those conclusions. My father loved talking with all types of people. He was such a good listener. He easily became friends with people very different from him. Why is mutual love so important? Because we were not called to be the Savior of the world. Jesus already did that. We are called to imitate Christ so that others can be drawn to Him.

LET'S DO LUNCH

My Nana, my father's mother, recently told me a story about when he was sick in the hospital just before he died. People had come in and out of his room all day, visiting between his physical therapy appointments. He was tired from all of the visitors and therapy, so he slept some of the afternoon. An African American girl with a mohawk stopped by to visit and asked for them to tell him that his niece came by. She explained that they call him Uncle Dave. He had hired her and trained her and some others. She said every couple of months, he takes them out to lunch and asks them how things are going or if they need any help. While dining at a local sandwich shop, Sid's, two men came by, and my father introduced her as his niece (I would guess he wanted to see their reactions). My father saw people in all their differences and loved all those differences mutually as he would someone that looked and acted just like him. His love for people was one of the most equalizing forces I have ever seen in this world. If you were loved by David Paul, you were his equal.

My father's lunch conversations would touch the lives of his friends, coworkers, family, youths, and former youths who had grown up, and even the parents of youth. This form of love is often looked over, and can be one of the hardest forms because it requires the person doing the loving thing outside of what they would want and how they think the person should live their life. This truly embodied the idea that a listening ear may not be revolutionary, but it is important. Coming face to face with others is about seeing them as the creation they were made as and loving them in that moment. What better way to be in communion with someone than over a meal?

Chapter 4

Equal Regard

> Love your neighbor and hate your enemy? No. Love
> your enemy and pray for those that persecute you.
> —Matthew 5:43–45

Gene Outka, a Yale ethicist, argued that Christian love should be defined as equal regard, which "means that we value all persons equally, regardless of their special traits, actions, merits, or what they can do for us" (*Kingdom Ethics*, p. 112). We may show love to different people in different ways, but the need to show love to all people loving them equally is a step to becoming Love. This is reflected in Christ's act to die for all people, which in turn gives equal regard to all people. This is no room for partiality.

Have you ever been driving and coming to a stop light where there is a person holding a handmade sign asking for help? I am sure the resounding answer is yes. If not all of us, many of us are familiar with this scene. What are our first reactions in this scene? Maybe if we pretend they are not there, they will not talk to us. Maybe we are praying the light changes before we have to make eye contact. Maybe we feel contempt because they obviously have issues with handling money to be in this position. Or maybe they are lying and are trying to scam us. Those are a lot of thoughts spiraling around in our minds during a sixty-second-long red light. Usually I am just trying to belt out my favorite line of the song I am listening to.

LET'S DO LUNCH

Why are we flooded with these thoughts at the sight of someone that seems desperate enough to stand in the weather and ask for help? We have been immersed in a society that categorizes people. Our society places value on the lives of people in different categories based on what we think they deserve. We treat each other on the basis of fairness we have cultivated as a society. Is it fair for someone to receive something that they did not work for? Is it fair for the government to give my hard-earned money to people that do not work as long or as hard as I do? Is it fair for people to use guilt to get what they want from me? What if fairness is not the point of life?

Loving people with equal regard is not just giving people space to do what they want. Loving people with equal regard is valuing all people equally. There is that word again, value. Just above, we were asking why do we change the value of someone in our society? Maybe the question should be "Why do we think value changes?"

Human beings tend to place value on something based on what good it does. A remote control with working batteries is more valuable than a remote control without working batteries. A car with an engine has way more value than a car without an engine. The problem with this value scale is that we place it also on human beings. Human beings are not objects we create to complete a task. Humans are not a placeholder for when a better version or edition is created. Human beings are made in the image of God. They have feelings, emotions, traumas, mistakes, joys, and capacity to love and give love. God has given humans the ability to have complex lives and to have choices for those lives. With all of those complexities in mind, how can we determine that someone's value has changed? So what would life look like if we valued all human life equally and did not treat others according to our scale of fairness? I think it would look a lot like Jesus.

My father made it his goal to teach his youth and all of us to value all human life. He was a juvenile probation officer and worked downtown. Working every weekday downtown, he came across many people asking for help and people experiencing homelessness. I was never taught that someone asking for money was trying to scam me. I was never taught that the person asking for help is probably an addict and will waste any assistance they are given. I was taught to value all human life. One aspect of that lesson was not even known to me until after he passed away. I was told that my father would carry his debit card for himself but would also carry cash every day. The cash was not for himself; instead it was for anyone that needed it or anyone that asked him. To him, everyone person he met was created in the image of God, and he treated them as such. He often said it was not his place to decide what the person would do with the money given; it was his place to give.

Before my father was a minister and reverend, he was loving people wildly. He suffered a great tragedy at the age of sixteen years old. His father died by suicide on Father's Day. After that day, it would just be my father, his mother, and his sister. My father was the younger sibling but often took care of many other people. He took care of them not to get a reward or praise but because he knew they needed someone to care for and love them. He was able to see a need that he could fill for those in pain. He was always looking for ways for God to use him instead of just waiting around for instructions. He did this during one of the most difficult parts of his life. During this time, he did not like God. He was mad at God for the pain they were going through since his father's death. The most miraculous thing was that my father was open to letting God use him even when he did not like God. Dad may not have understood that God was working through him, but God never missed a beat in the midst of my father's pain.

My father was a part of a group for boys called the DeMolay. It was a Masonic group for young boys. One of the boys my father knew from that group called him one evening after my father got home from high school. The boy said he was going to run away from home and asked where he should go. My father drove over thirty minutes to his house to talk to the boy and his family. This was the time before cell phones, so no one knew where he was; just that he left home at six thirty in the evening. My grandmother was pretty upset but knew my father had done the right thing. He knew it would be a better idea to talk to this boy rather than just let him run away. Dad held this boy in equal regard to himself because he knew the boy needed someone to care about what he was going through.

The DeMolays had a girl group called the Rainbows. One of the girls from the Rainbows asked my father to talk to her friend that had just lost her dad. She knew that my father had experience with this and would be a good person for this girl to talk to. By this time, my father was in college but made time to talk with her and spend time with her and her family. They never dated, but again, he knew she needed someone to care about what she was going through. He asked his mother and sister if they could all go to Six Flags, and she could come with them. He continually kept up with her and her grandparents that she was now living with, even sharing Sunday lunches with them. My father did not just "talk the talk." He walked right alongside people and regarded them as equals that needed someone to care about them. His pain helped him see that so many were also in pain and needed love.

My father would eventually be ordained as a reverend and was a juvenile probation officer. He could be called Reverend Paul, Mr. Paul, or even Mr. David Paul. All of these titles he earned and wore as a blessing. But the best title of all was Dave. His friends, youth groups, and others he would help knew him as Dave, just Dave. No fancy titles. No accolades. He never thought of himself as better than anyone else even with the titles he earned. He was best known as Dave because that is who he was to everyone who interacted with him. He was their equal. I did not always understand this as a child because I only knew him as Daddy" or David Paul when he had to fill out papers for school for me. While I never asked him before he passed, I would bet that being called Dave was one of the most honorable titles he was called here on earth.

Thinking of others with equal regard can change your life. You become someone that does not anger as easily or gets frustrated as easily. You become someone that understands that they cannot possibly understand the different experiences of all the people around you. One of the qualities I loved about my father was his need to encourage others to step up in their walk with Christ to be the loving child of God they were created to be. Some may not have loved that characteristic because he would step on a lot of toes while reminding people to give up their own interests for the interests of others (Galatians). When my father came across people that claimed to be followers of Christ but would put people down and judge people on one interaction, my father would become frustrated, and it showed. He would not back down to people that had an idea of not caring for others like Christ cares for them.

I have recently become a therapist and just finished my master's degree in clinical mental health counseling. I have seen more and more over the past years in school that my father's desire to become a counselor after he retired were right on target. I have just discussed how my father lived a life of equal regard. One of the most important lessons I learned in counseling school was unconditional positive regard.

> "Our goal [as counselors] is to care unconditionally for clients, to listen to what they say without judgment, and to be warm and caring. It is important not to judge clients but rather to understand how they have gotten to be as they are" (Clara E. Hill, *Helping Skills*, p. 34).

As counselors, it is very important for the trust of the client to not approach a situation with judgment. The people we serve should know that what they are experiencing is important and that they can trust the person they are opening up to. I sat in class reading these words immediately knowing that I have seen this way of living before, through my dad.

Equal regard changes how we respond to others because we truly want to treat them as we would want to be treated. Equal regard takes away stipulations we place on others to present why they are deserving of help or understanding. I will no longer see the world as a system of scales of values because of my father.

CHAPTER 5

Delivering Love
Love by Delivering from Oppression

> Love by delivering from oppression.
> —David Gushee

David Gushee describes delivering love stating "that love is not just a single principle, like a song sung in a monotone, but a complex drama, with different dramatic actions as the characters grow and interact" (*Kingdom Ethics*, p. 113). This brings Gushee to the four crucial acts in the drama of delivering love, including that "love sees with compassion and enters into the situation of persons in bondage, love does deeds of deliverance, love invites into community with freedom, justice, and responsibility for the future, and love confronts those who exclude" (*Kingdom Ethics*, pp. 115–118). Delivering love is again not about the giver but about those in need. It is not about pulling the oppressed up, but going down to where the oppressed are, entering into their situation. Delivering love delivers from oppression not with the motivation to look good to others, but with the motivation of loving others so much you wish to understand what they are going through and walk that path with them. I think this is why my father was drawn to counseling, and I think that is why I have been given the passion of helping others through counseling myself. It is not about my father but about the voices he raised up.

Stand in the gap: unconditional positive regard is defined by humanistic psychologists to mean expressing empathy, support, and acceptance to someone regardless of what they say or do.

As I mentioned before, I recently graduated with a master's degree in clinical mental health counseling from Fort Valley State University, and we learned about the skills a counselor has to possess in order to best serve their clients. Diving further into the idea of unconditional positive regard, it is important to notice that clients dealing with other society, hurt, and anxiety may not be able to be fully present in counseling. We may have to set aside the counseling conversation in order to stand in the gap for them. Get them resources to be able to get to their job (bus passes). Get them to another resource that can help with the issue weighing on them. We as counselors must seek to understand our clients in more than just the way we see them. My father constantly stood in the gap with others. He stood before judges wanting to throw the book at youth teens in trouble, but my father spoke to the judge and stood up for those teens in order for them to work through their issues and grow. My father and mother bought groceries for a youth that was thrown out of her home because of the person she was dating. My father even intervened spiritually by constantly praying for and interceding on the behalf of others facing trauma, addictions, and sorrow. There was a short video that made its way around social media of two young children that looked like they were in a flooded urban area. There was fast water running through a cement walkway, blocking the path of the children. The little boy crossed first and became a bridge for the little girl to cross on top of. My mother shared that video because she immediately saw my dad as that little boy. My dad would stand in the gap, in the valley, or in the chasm for another person to get to safety, feel loved, or find the path to Christ. He understood Jesus's call to all those that follow Him to "pick up their cross and follow me" (Matthew 16:24).

I once saw this movie called *Hacksaw Ridge*, which focused on the World War II experience of Desmond Doss, an American pacifist combat medic who, as a Seventh-day Adventist Christian, refused to carry or use a weapon or firearm of any kind. Doss was the first conscientious objector to be awarded the Medal of Honor for service above and beyond the call of duty during the Battle of Okinawa. After the initial fight with major loss on both sides of the Americans and the Japanese upon Hacksaw Ridge, the Japanese launched a massive counterattack, leaving many Americans wounded and stranded.

Doss ascended onto the ridge and hears one of his comrades and was able to covertly bring him to safety. Doss had a choice: he can go with the comrade he has brought to safety, or he can go back for anyone else. Doss heard another that is still alive and decides to reenter the battleground. Doss prayed, "Lord, help me get one more. Just one more!" Doss continued to hear the cries of the wounded and was able to carry out seventy-five wounded soldiers and belay them down to safety without carrying a firearm.

God did not call Doss to save an entire battalion, and Doss did not enter the battlefield with the idea that he was going to be the unit's savior. He just asked for one more. God does not call us to be the savior of the entire population of unbelievers. God calls us to one. One person at a time that we stop and listen to hear their pain and bring them to the Healer. I saw this same behavior from my father throughout his ministry. There were possibly hundreds of people at my father's funeral. Is that an indication that my father was a "savior" or a pastor of a megachurch? Not at all. My father discipled people one at a time, one-on-one, listening to their pain and struggles, then lifting their voices, meeting their needs, and showing them the love and power of the Healer. My father was not a war hero. He was obedient. He showed us that love and service speak the same language.

I have never been truly oppressed. Google defines oppression as "prolonged cruel or unjust treatment or control." I have been made fun of for the way I looked, my level of intelligence, and my "goody-goody" nature. While being made fun of has never been okay or good, I have not been through prolonged cruel or unjust treatment. Because I have not truly experienced oppression, I must seek the voices of those that have to find how my life can help.

Why should I seek the voices of those that are oppressed? What if I do not think they are oppressed, or maybe I think they should work to get out of that oppression themselves? Love works to deliver those out of oppression. But does that make the deliverer a savior? This is why it is important to listen to the voices of those oppressed. Living a life of active delivering love is not about being a savior. Being active in delivering love looks more like using one's gifts to lift up the lives and voices of others. We must remember that delivering love does not work without equal regard. We must find equal value in those that are oppressed to not place ourselves as the savior. There is only one that can truly heal and save people, and that person is Jesus. We are called to reflect Jesus, but we must remember we are not Him and cannot save people. Delivering love is only love when it holds the oppressed as equals.

There are some that seek to embody delivering love to make yourself feel better. When we help someone we feel like is in a worse position than us, we can feel more important and like better people. The interesting part about our call to follow Jesus is that Jesus always focused on making oneself lower while raising others up. This means that if we want to embody delivering love, it must be about seeing the value in others and seeing that our world has harmed those others and then doing what we can to rectify the growing dehumanization.

Our world is full of people that sin and hurt each other. As humans, our track record of treating each other well is not a great record. Jesus had a love for those the world seemed to hate or ignore. He seemed to work hard to help people see that their future could be different from the world intended for them. While Jesus delivered us all from the punishment of sin and death, we can reflect this type of love. We can begin this embodiment by sitting with anyone that has been harmed or hurt by others. No matter what that looks like and even if we are not supposed to "like" them. Listening to people up close tends to melt away any preconceived notions we may have.

My father showed me how to embody delivering love in ways I didn't even know. The summer after he passed away, we were invited to a program at a girls' summer camp in town. This camp was for girls ages twelve to seventeen to teach interview skills and coping skills and to encourage them through things they are passionate about. We were invited to the end of the summer program because this camp was created with the help of my father.

LET'S DO LUNCH

As a juvenile probation officer, he understood the complicated issues that can change the trajectory of a teenager's life. He saw what abuse, being trapped in low income, and cycles of emotional abuse could do to the future of a teen. He also had an excellent understanding that he was not their savior. He was not there to be what they needed in life. He was there to be a path for them to find true love and acceptance through Jesus and to do that through a future apart from the trauma they had experienced.

Public schools often have dress code rules for graduation. You must wear a certain type of dress, pants, shirt, and shoes. If a student does not have the correct clothing, they are not allowed to walk across the stage on graduation day. My father, as a youth pastor and juvenile probation officer, knew that if a student worked hard to make it to graduation, they deserved to walk across the stage. I was told after his death that he bought countless pairs of shoes for those students that could not afford the correct ones for the ceremony. This was not an advertised action. I had no idea he would do this while it was happening. He was a minister, worked for the state, and my mother was a substitute teacher and church administrative assistant. We would not have been counted as a family with money, but my father made sure that if a student made it to graduation, they would get to walk.

Embodying delivering love is a tough way to live. It means looking at those and speaking to those the world would tell you to ignore. It means getting to know people the world has told you are evil who do not deserve to be valued. It means risking relationships with people that may not understand why you care so much. It means risking your money or time on people that may not be appreciative.

My father's father committed suicide when my father was sixteen years old. The act was committed on Father's Day. I think my father reached out to people so well because he understood going through trauma at a young age. He understood being angry and not wanting anything to do with God. But what is truly amazing is that he knew he was created to love others well even if he was angry with God. During the next few years after the death of his father, my father became a safe haven for the neighborhood kids. He always made sure those around him had someone looking out for them.

Embodying delivering love means a life of being able to look through the filter of sadness and trauma and still walking beside others that are hurting.

As I mentioned in the Introduction, my father was not perfect. He often pushed aside his needs in order to help others. While this could be seen as sacrificial love from chapter 2, it can also be damaging. My grandmother told me that when he was in his early years in college, he was taking care of a girl that had a lot of mental health issues and drove her to a mental health clinic. He stayed in the waiting room and never once cared who may have seen him there. He put her needs first before thinking of himself. This is significant because of what he told me over twenty-five years later that he put off seeking mental healthcare for his trauma until his forties. He always knew when others needed to seek guidance but often put their needs first. He told me he should not have waited so long to seek help. I remembered this when he passed away, and I sought help with my mental health to deal with his death.

PART 2
IN ACTION

Chapter 6

Can We Embody Love? A Transformed Life

But the fruit of the Spirit is love, joy, peace, patience, kindness, goodness, faithfulness, gentleness, self-control; against such things there is no law.
—Galatians 5:22–23

By this all people will know that you are my disciples, if you have love for one another.
—John 13:35

This is the part I have felt is missing in so many books. We must know how to do this. We have now learned about the definitions of love, how important these definitions are, and how they work together. You must then wonder, *How do I do it? How can I let go of my human instinct to live for myself, hold grudges, pass judgments, and withhold forgiveness?* Can we *really* do this? We must make a conscious decision every single day to walk in love. That's right! This is not a one-stop shop of how to love. This is a plea for a daily conscious decision to turn away from ourselves and to turn toward others.

But why can't we just snap our fingers and become loving people? Because love is not a cup of Folgers. It is not instant. If you have ever fallen in love with another person, you know that love may start in a moment but is not sustained in just one moment. The kind of love that we have defined in this book cannot be sustained through one, single decision to love. Sacrificial love is not manifested by one sacrifice. What happens when the person we must sacrifice for does not love us, is not appreciative, or is a hateful person? The decision to love must be consciously made each time. Sacrificial love, mutual love, equal regard, and delivering love work together through intentional actions. When these intentional actions are made daily, you can actually become Love.

When my mom found the book my father was writing, she printed out what he had written and gave it to me as a college graduation present. After finding it, she also found a quote I mentioned in chapter 2: "Give freely of yourself, your love, your life." She told me she had no idea where he heard it, but it was important enough to type out and save. If someone were to have asked him why he saved that quote, I think he would have said that he hoped he could live his life by that quote. The interesting part that all that knew him witnessed is that he embodied this quote better than most people anyone knew. And I think that is the secret, those that are embodying Love do not follow a booklet of "how to." They make daily decisions that their life will no longer be centered on themselves but instead will be about others. When we think that we have finally figured out how to embody love and become like Jesus, that is the moment we have stopped making love the center.

Becoming Love also includes our motivation. Motivation is the secret to everything we do. Many of our daily actions come from the motivation of routine. As humans, we enjoy routine and work best in it. Another common motivation is obligation. We do not always want to do the things necessary in this world. Show up when we are not in the mood. Give gifts on certain days of the year. See people we have not seen in forever. One motivation for all of these actions could be obligation. We feel obligated to show the world we are "that" kind of person. The thoughtful person, kind person, and a grateful person. Obligation goes against our human need to be selfish. But it also is the opposite of being Kingdom-minded.

What does it mean to be Kingdom-minded? The other day I thought about the great debate I have seen for years. Would Jesus have been Republican or Democrat? We want our thoughts, opinions, and convictions to be confirmed so much that we hope and pray Jesus looked like us. But we have it backwards. We are supposed to look like Jesus. Jesus was not Republican minded. Jesus was not Democrat minded. Jesus was not Libertarian minded. Jesus was not even totally politically minded. While he made political moves, made statements that might lean one way or another, Jesus was always Kingdom-minded. Jesus's motivation was for God's Kingdom to be on earth. Since we are not perfect but instead are sinful creatures, Jesus became the sacrifice so that we might be one step closer to being Kingdom-minded and a path to the Father.

How do we know if we have become Kingdom-minded? They will know us by our love and our fruit. One of my favorite analogies Jesus uses to explain how to become his disciples is to examine what kind of "fruit" we are producing. There is always an outward reflection of how we live our lives; what comes out of our life from how we have lived. This is explained as the fruit which we bear. Our fruit, like the fruit from a tree, is visible for all to see. We can clearly see if a tree is infected or is no longer producing fruit at all. This is the same with our lives. It is clearly visible if we are producing the fruit of the Spirit, which includes love, joy, peace, patience, kindness, goodness, faithfulness, gentleness, and self-control. When we decide to become Love, we cannot just embody a loving nature. We must be so full of all these characteristics that it is clearly visible to those around us.

My friend and college roommate, Casey Wayne, wrote a devotional called *Abundant Fruit*. She dove into each of these characteristics listed above and how we can show them in our lives. This is it! This is how we do it! When a decision comes up in our lives of what to do, we ask,

"What can I do to be loving?"
"What can I do that brings joy?"
"What can I say that brings peace?"
"What can I do to show patience?"
"What can I say to show kindness?"

"What can I do to show God's goodness?"
"What can I practice that shows faithfulness?"
"What can I do that shows gentleness?"
"What can I do to exhibit self-control?"

Each of these questions are intentional and are not one-time-only questions. We must ask these questions daily in order to live a life of love. I think that this is the point where many of us bow out. This is the hard, day-in and day-out work. We choose to be loving when we are hurt. We choose to look for joy when we are in the valley. We choose to bring peace when we are baited into hostility. We choose to have patience when we have waited longer than we ever thought we could. We choose to be kind when it is so easy to cut someone down with our words. We choose to show God's goodness to those we deem evil. We choose to be faithful to God when we are tempted to chase our desires. We choose to be gentle when our frustration is at its highest. We choose to have self-control when we are surrounded by chaos. We get to decide what fruit we produce for the world to see. We get to choose.

David Paul chose what kind of fruit he would produce. He chose multiple thankless jobs to help those the world has forgotten. He chose to celebrate life even though he has more than enough reasons to hate this world. He chose to mediate rather than to blame. He chose to spend over twenty-five years working with teenagers who regularly ignored his advice and support. He chose to give what little money he had to someone that had none. He chose to let his life be a testimony for others to see what God can do. He chose to respond to tension with quiet consolation. He chose to not participate in much this world offers to show that only Jesus satisfies.

While you may be thinking, *Wow! David Paul clearly showed perfect fruit!* Let's remember he was also human. He sometimes yelled when he was overwhelmed. He lost patience with teenagers that laughed through Bible lessons. He had moments of cynicism and sarcasm that could be hurtful to others. He had years of doubting the goodness of God. My father clearly produced heavenly fruit, but not all of the branches were healthy. They can't be. We are all broken and live in a broken world. He did not let these moments of bad fruit be the end of his story. This is why God allows us to be pruned.

Pruning is the act of cutting off dead branches and leaves on a plant to give room for a healthy, new fruit. I have seen someone cut off nearly every branch and leaf, leaving a pretty sad-looking "plant," which I would not even call it a plant at that point. Then days to weeks later, beautiful new buds have appeared! The plant was cut down to give room for new growth. This isn't just some cute Sunday School metaphor. Jesus taught it!

"Every branch in me that does not bear fruit he takes away, and every branch that does bear fruit he prunes, that it may bear more fruit" (John 15:2).

God sees the branches or parts of our lives that are not bearing good fruit and allows for a season of pruning to give room for new growth. Pruning is not an easy process. Pruning can be painful, seemingly unjust, unfair, and with no explanation. We may see a pruning of something we thought was good fruit like a ministry we thought we were doing for the glory of God, but in fact, we were enjoying the praise of a job well done. A life that is working to become Love is a transformed life of new growth. Trust God through the pruning.

Chapter 7

Will We Embody Love? A Choice Must be Made

> When Jesus heard this, he marveled and said to those who followed him, "'Truly, I tell you, with no one in Israel have I found such faith."
> —Matthew 8:10

We have seen the four definitions of love. We have seen it through the life of David Paul, through the teachings of Jesus, and we have seen how we can do it ourselves. The next question to wrestle with is "Will we?" God gives us the choice to live however we see fit. We get to decide if we want to become Love. Will we? How do we decide to live a life becoming Love?

Trauma has a way of changing our trajectory. This theme is weaved throughout scripture, history, movies, books, and even our lives. Not every single person will face a moment of intense trauma, but our world is broken, leaving trauma to enter our lives in any number of ways. How can love persevere in a world full of trauma? How can one's trajectory in life be grounded in love when trauma and brokenness exist at an alarming rate? How can we embody love when our lives embody pain? A choice must be made.

As I mentioned in chapter 4, my father lost his dad at a young age to suicide. Not only did his family have to process their loved one taking his own life, they also had to process that he did it on Father's Day. This type of pain cannot be explained with words. Only those that have experienced such deep trauma can start to understand. This was not revealed to me until I was in high school. I look back on my life at all the Father's Days past knowing that day held so much pain for my father. I know the pain of losing my father but not at such a young age and not with the added trauma of how and when.

As I write this, I have recently finished my master's degree in clinical mental health counseling and am a full-time therapist. I am also in the middle of writing this book and will be a speaker at a teen girls' conference this year. How did I get here? Tragedy. The tragedy and pure shock of losing my father before I graduated college changed everything about my life. Not only have I been able to sympathize with those that are grieving, but I can also really empathize with them. I have seen their pain just like my father understood that pain. The only way my trajectory landed me here, a therapist trying to be a writer, was that tragedy.

Knowing somewhat of the pain he felt, I cannot imagine how much strength it took for my father to live a life of love. He did not have to choose to walk beside people in their pain, watching them in their sorrow, holding them as they cried, and loving them through their trauma. Each person he took time to get to know was a significant choice that he made intentionally. This is the power of Love; the Love which has a name, Jesus. I want to be able to show that the tragedy that changed my trajectory including molding me into becoming Love.

Recently, my mother was talking to me about my ordination and what this event means for my life. After graduating from seminary school with a master's degree in divinity, working on staff at a church as a youth pastor, and interning as a chaplain with a ministry in Atlanta, serving those experiencing homelessness, I made the decision to move to become ordained as a reverend. My father was also ordained, which is important to understand his motivations to choose to become Love.

Until recently, my ordination felt like another step to becoming a counselor. It felt like the necessary step to take after my history ministering to youth and others for fourteen years. Talking with my mother helped me see that my ordination was anything but just a step. My ordination was a celebration of my answer to God's call for me to be set apart from others. From this moment forward, my future, career, family, and actions are no longer mine to decide. My path is now laid out by God's calling. No matter what jobs, career path, or ministries I do in the future, I cannot sway from where God is calling me.

A way to explain this would be to compare it to a movie scene. The movie *Risen* is an American biblical drama film that details a Roman soldier's search for Yeshua's body following his resurrection (Wikipedia). The Roman soldier follows the disciples to Galilee where they are to meet Jesus after the resurrection. He sees their interactions with the risen Christ, shocked at what he is witnessing. Jesus explains to the disciples that they are to now become fishers of men and go and exclaim His glory throughout the nations. The disciples start to leave when the soldier pulls one aside and asks, "So after all of this, you will just go and do as He says?" The disciple answers, "How can we do anything else?" Once Christ has called you out to become Love, you cannot possibly do anything else. The pull, need, desire, and fulfillment upon one's life is irrefutable. One must follow through as it has become one's purpose of living.

Do we actually want to become Love? We must change our motivation. While I would love for this book to take off and sell out, I also know that it may never leave my community. And that's okay. Being compelled to live a life of love is not pride deep or even ministry deep. It is a soul-deep need to show people that they truly matter. I am currently reading Hannah Brencher's memoir, *If You Find This Letter: My Journey to Find Purpose Through Hundreds of Letters to Strangers*. I cannot believe this book was written over seven years ago, and I am just now reading it! Her words echo the longing of my heart to create a world, a way of living, where people around me know they are loved. While Hannah searched for purpose serving in New York City (Wow! Man, am I jealous!), she fell in love with an idea—the idea of leaving love letters all around the city in an attempt to show people they matter. She told people to email her if they wanted a love letter, and she received hundreds of requests. Hundreds of people needed to know someone cared.

And that was ten years ago.

I wonder how many more would ask a complete stranger to send them a love letter in the desperation of feeling known. In the age of instant gratification, easy meals in minutes, messaging someone across the world in an instant, seeing global news in real time, and getting instant dopamine highs when your post is "liked" or seen. In a world of instant, why do hundreds, if not thousands, still feel unknown, not seen, and not loved? Connection may be the easiest; it has been in history, but deep, human connection still struggles. Becoming Love is more than being a nice person. It is living intentionally for others to know they are seen. When we become Love, people automatically feel known because they are getting a tiny glimpse of the Love that created them. We live in order to give ourselves away, just as Jesus did. While we can never do this perfectly as Jesus, we should feel compelled to try. But why do we not feel compelled to spread love?

See, my father, as a follower of Christ, had every chance to choose something else but chose to answer the call of his Master. He worked long hours, finishing college as a newlywed while working. He planned to become a lawyer, being able to provide for his family and to not have to worry about money. He was greatly disappointed when he was turned down for law school. His visions of nice things for his family began to disappear from his hopes. While we never had much money as a family, my father's life path saved lives and gave hope to countless people throughout his twenty-five-year ministry. He may not have chosen the path that seemed wise or what the world would see as successful, but once he was called by Christ, he could do nothing else. If we truly give ourselves over to becoming Love, we can do nothing else because imitating God's divine love will become your identity.

Chapter 8

Imitators of More than Love

> One common reason we fail to leave sin behind is that
> we have a domesticated view of Jesus... We have a
> domesticated view that, for all its doctrinal precision,
> has downsized the glory of Christ in our hearts.
> —Dane Ortlund, *Deeper*, p.21

> Therefore, be imitators of God, as beloved children.
> And walk in love, as Christ loved us and gave himself
> up for us, a fragrant offering and sacrifice to God.
> —Ephesians 5:1–2

We have now decided that we can embody love and that we will embody love, but have we taken the time to realize that there is more to imitating Jesus? Becoming Love is a daily decision that involves more than loving others as we have found. Jesus's entire being is love, meaning He cannot cease to love or He would be no more. We have just begun to see how deep Jesus's love truly is, and if we are to imitate this love and work to become Love, we should understand how deep this love goes.

    Dane Ortlund is the author of *Gentle and Lowly* and *Deeper*, two books that discuss the character of Jesus and how we can know Jesus deeper. Ortlund lays the foundation to knowing Jesus more in *Deeper* by discussing Jesus Christ's fullness, our emptiness, and our union with Him. He takes a look at seven facets of Jesus: ruling, saving, befriending, preserving, interceding, returning, and tenderness. Jesus is able to embody these characteristics perfectly. Jesus, being divine and human, showed us how to be Kingdom-minded in the most perfect way. He could not falter in any facet of His character. He was perfectly compassionate, the perfect Savior, the perfect friend, perfectly tender. Also, Jesus did not just display these characteristics one at a time. He intertwined them deeper into the perfect display of Love. The best part of the foundation Ortlund laid was though we cannot be perfectly in character of Jesus, we can be in union with Jesus.

I think my father worked to become Love before he ever knew what that fully meant. He was willing to continually search for God's heart and imitate the love he found. When he would falter in his imitation of Jesus, he would apologize and work to know Jesus deeper to continue working to become Love. One of the best ways my father was able to imitate Jesus to work to become Love was in his friendships. Ortlund writes,

> What does a friend do? A friend draws near in time of need. A friend delights to come into solidarity with us, bearing our burdens. A friend listens. A friend is available to us, never too high or important to give us time. (*Deeper*, p. 28)

My father was excellent at drawing near to others. He gave others space to talk through their thoughts and feelings and did not hold his own life or time above someone else's. This is why *Let's Do Lunch* has this title; Dad made space for anyone and everyone he could over a meal through a phone call, through email. No person was below him or a waste of his time. He had a fascinating way of helping others knowing they were not inferior but held the dignity of their image of God as human. He was even learning to intertwine these characteristics while working to become Love.

One example of how my father would intertwine these characteristics would be intertwining, befriending, and interceding. The longer I have gone without my father, the more stories of his interceding are revealed. I have been told of my father standing up for his youth in court, advocating for them to their parents and other authorities and even setting aside his time and health to sit with them and their family during devastation.

My father was one of the best advocates for adolescents I have ever known. He would take time to get to know all of the youth in his care as a juvenile probation officer or youth pastor and would use that knowledge of who they really were to advocate for their future. He knew when one of his youths needed someone to steer them in the right direction because he knew their heart and their potential. He never saw them as projects to fix, but as people to love.

My father spent countless hours sitting in hospitals. He would sit with family as their loved ones were in surgery, fighting for their lives, or recovering. He would listen, encourage, pray, laugh, and weep with those that needed it most. He made sure to make time for any family that was in the hospital, so they would know they were loved and cared for. Even when he could not fix anything in their situation, he did not look away or pretend he did not see their suffering. He moved in closer as a friend.

Story time!

As we have discussed, my father was a youth pastor. He went through so many years of working with youth groups, some numbering thirty to fifty youths and others maybe just eight. During the times when there were too many youths to count, he would ask the church to hire an intern. A few of these interns later turned into people working to become Love, and I think Dad knew that about them and saw that potential in them. One of those interns served with my father for a few years then decided to go to seminary school. Her school and future career in the ministry stopped short after it was discovered she had a benign brain tumor and needed surgery.

As it turns out, my father had just had a surgery himself to remove polyps on his vocal cords with the strict instructions to not speak for four to six weeks in order for his vocal cords to heal. The moment he heard of his intern needing emergency surgery, we left the house to be with the family in the hospital. There was no question in his mind. He did use his voice some during this time and later, because of other reasons, he needed to have the surgery to remove the polyps again, but I know there is not a single regret in his mind that he did what God called him to do. He sat with her family, praying, interceding, and encouraging them as she went through surgery. He would continue to love and laugh with this family as his intern and friend worked to heal.

How did my father learn to live like this? How can one man choose to live a life in search for those that need to know Jesus, that need to see Love? He imitated Jesus, his Savior. Jesus came not only to save us from the penalty of sin in order to reconcile us to God but also to show us how to be Kingdom-minded and begin the Kingdom of God on earth. It was important for humanity to see God's Kingdom through the life of a human that we could work to imitate. One of the best examples of this was Jesus's friendships with His disciples.

> Greater love has no one than this, that someone lays down his life for his friends. You are my friends if you do what I command you. No longer do I call you servants, for the servant does not know what his master is doing; but I have called you friends, for all that I have heard from my Father I have made known to you. (John 15:13–15 ESV)

Jesus did not wander through Israel on His own, preaching and teaching and hoping people would follow Him. Jesus was baptized by John the Baptist and consecrated (set apart) by God, tempted in the wilderness as a way to grow in His relationship with God and prove his sinless life, then immediately called his disciples. Did he need twelve men that were just minding their own business and fishing or doing their jobs? No! Jesus, as we have discussed, was perfectly God and presented perfect love, compassion, interceding, and more. Jesus did not need sinful, worldly men for his ministry. But He called them, and they were not only his students but also his friends. He showed them how to love like a friend, encourage and support like a friend. Jesus was not their master standing over them. He ate with them, reclined with them, and communed with them. He grew in closeness with them so that they would know and understand that He is Love.

I think we can get friendship wrong sometimes in the Christian world. We forget to look at how Jesus taught us to be a friend in His Kingdom. Jesus repeatedly taught the disciples and followers the same lessons over and over. He did not give up on them when they could not understand and did not lose faith that they would work to become Love. These acts of love by Jesus bring me to one of my favorite verses, "Now before the Feast of the Passover, when Jesus knew that his hour had come to depart out of this world to the Father, having loved his own who were in the world, he loved them to the end" (John 13:1 ESV).

Jesus knew the time had come to show the first definition of Love: sacrificing His own life to cover the sins of the world. The interesting part was Jesus did not place Himself into the role of a martyr, but a tender and loving friend. He had taught, led, loved, and encouraged His friends for a few years by this point and knew that His crucifixion would be incredibly hard and confusing for them. Rather than leaving the disciples with a vague story of what was going to happen, He loved them and stayed with them to the very end. It would have been easy for Jesus to leave them behind and get on with His sacrifice, but He could not leave them in such darkness. He took time to wash their feet, show them how to serve others, and explain that this path was going to be very hard but also the best decision they had ever made. He encouraged them by saying, "I have said these things to you, that in me you may have peace. In the world you will have tribulation. But take heart; I have overcome the world" (John 16:33 ESV).

Seeing Jesus love His disciples with such compassion and tenderness encourages me to not give up on others that struggle to follow Jesus's ways. It can be easy to leave people behind that refuse to even try becoming Love or who constantly let the darkness of the world overtake them. But Jesus loved them to the end. We cannot give up just because the path gets hard. We must ask Jesus for help when we want to give up. The best part about learning to become Love is that we get to ask Love for help.

> If you love me, you will keep my commandments. And I will ask the Father, and he will give you another Helper,[a] to be with you forever, even the Spirit of truth, whom the world cannot receive, because it neither sees him nor knows him. You know him, for he dwells with you and will be in you. (John 14:15–17 ESV)

Jesus not only loved the disciples to the end but also asked God to give them and all believers the Holy Spirit, our Helper, to be with us always in His place. We are not left to fend for ourselves or try to become Love out of our own strength and efforts. We have been given God Himself to encourage us, remind us of the Truth, and to strengthen us as we work to imitate Jesus and become Love.

I am reminded of the message my father gave after he was called from Mt. Pleasant Baptist Church to be a youth pastor at Musella Baptist Church. He spoke on a passage in Philippians.

> So if there is any encouragement in Christ, any comfort from love, any participation in the Spirit, any affection and sympathy, complete my joy by being of the same mind, having the same love, being in full accord and of one mind. Do nothing from selfish ambition or conceit, but in humility count others more significant than yourselves. Let each of you look not only to his own interests, but also to the interests of others. Have this mind among yourselves, which is yours in Christ Jesus, who, though he was in the form of God, did not count equality with God a thing to be grasped, but emptied himself, by taking the form of a servant, being born in the likeness of

men. And being found in human form, he humbled himself by becoming obedient to the point of death, even death on a cross. Therefore God has highly exalted him and bestowed on him the name that is above every name, so that at the name of Jesus every knee should bow, in heaven and on earth and under the earth, and every tongue confess that Jesus Christ is Lord, to the glory of God the Father.

Therefore, my beloved, as you have always obeyed, so now, not only as in my presence but much more in my absence, work out your own salvation with fear and trembling, for it is God who works in you, both to will and to work for his good pleasure. (Philippians 2:1–13 ESV)

My father knew that the youth group at Mt. Pleasant Baptist Church may not understand why he had to leave their church as he was called to another church to serve as their youth pastor. He borrowed the words from Paul in Philippians about who Jesus is, what Jesus has done, and how the people in Philippi should work to become Love. My father spoke to the youth, that he hoped they would continue to work out their salvation and obedience in Jesus even in his absence. He did not leave them with a vague message or promises he could not keep. My father left them with the most important information, who is Love, and encouraged them to continue to become Love. He was with them to the end.

CHAPTER 9

You've Decided to Become Love, Now Have Some Fun!

> Live a Life of Love and Light.
> —Hannah Rule

The majority of this book sounds like a lot of hard work, doesn't it? Becoming a little more like Jesus means doing things with the Kingdom in a mindset, which is usually opposite of the world around us. But one of the best parts about becoming Love is that you get to spread *joy*! Heaven is filled with joy, worship, and no more tears. If we are working to build the Kingdom here and live Kingdom-minded, then we need to be bringing some joy! I'm not sure people would call my father whimsical or silly, but he sure did know how to laugh. Again, here are words from my father's best friend Brian remembering Dad's laugh on the tenth year of his passing:

> Ten years surely gone fast...yet so slow at the same time. The world recently remembered the death of Buddy Holly, the Big Bopper, and Ritchie Valens on Feb 3, 1959. A song was written about it entitled "The Day the Music Died." February 7, 2010, is what those of us who knew you would call the day the laughter died. David

Paul was probably the funniest person I have ever known. He wasn't a comedian or jokester, but it was as if God said, "You are going to make people laugh without even trying." I had someone ask me once, "Why does he look mad all the time?" I never had noticed until then, but I stepped back. Sure enough, I laughed again…David resembled a mafia boss. How funny, the one who cared more for people than anyone I've known, looked like a mafia boss. The best was when he laughed too. If he found something funny, that raspy laugh would ring out above anyone else. Yes, we have laughed again during these ten years… Just like the fact that the music was never the same after that fateful day, so laughter is never the same. There is just a hint of sadness that now echoes in our smiles. You caused us to laugh, just by your presence. You even allowed us to laugh at you sometimes, and you never got mad. Things have moved on, but they can never be the same. For now, we hear the echo of your raspy laugh as it rings out in heaven. One day…the laughter will truly be alive again! Looking forward to the day that our laughter is complete.

Until then, my friend…

My father knew how to laugh. He laughed when we were being silly kids. He laughed at his favorite show, *Seinfeld*. He laughed when he would embarrass his youth group. He would laugh with his sister while visiting in Blairsville over pretty much everything. He laughed, and he brought so much joy. He loved showing up for people in ways they never would have imagined. He would give them a ride when no one else would. He would show up to events just so a teenager or friend would have a familiar face in the crowd. He was the busiest man I have ever known but still found time to laugh and make others feel special. He may have looked like a stern mafia boss, but my father always got the joke and usually had another ready to go.

I believe that Jesus also liked to have fun. I don't think that he went to all those dinner parties just to teach people. Jesus loved to eat and fellowship. He loved to hear people's stories. He listened to endless questions. I don't think someone that loved to fellowship and be in communion with others so much was a party pooper. Jesus was able to connect with so many different people by celebrating them as children of God. Jesus even had breakfast with his friends after He was resurrected!

> When they got out on land, they saw a charcoal fire in place, with fish laid out on it, and bread. Jesus said to them, "Bring some of the fish that you have just caught." So Simon Peter went aboard and hauled the net ashore, full of large fish, 153 of them. And although there were so many, the net was not torn. Jesus said to them, "Come and have breakfast." Now none of the disciples dared ask him, "Who are you?" They knew it was the Lord. Jesus came and took the bread and gave it to them, and so with the fish. (John 21: 9–13 ESV)

Jesus knew that eating breakfast with His friends was exactly what they needed at that time. He did not choose to lecture them or tell them everything they were going to have to do. He had a bonfire with them! Can you imagine the laughter that rang out during that breakfast? The disciples were with their friend again! Their friend had died a terrible death and was now risen! I love imagining the smiles, hugs, and laughter that continued throughout that meal. Jesus liked to be present with others, if not all the time, but especially when he wanted to grow closer to them. I think Jesus was busy but knew in order to be in relationship with us, joy had to be a part of it.

One of my favorite authors that I mentioned in the Introduction does this so well. Bob Goff continually lives a life of whimsy. Bob throws love around like confetti and throws taffy from his dock to boaters at his Canadian cabin. Bob brings balloons wherever he goes because he knows one of the best parts about life is laughing. Now don't misunderstand me. Becoming Love in a world full of sin can be hard. Bob is a lawyer and used his gift to free child prisoners in Uganda. He knew that children were being hurt and exploited and knew that he had to do something about it. The doors of that prison are now hanging in Bob's office. Bob was able to bring freedom to hurting children through God's love and vision, and Bob has not stopped celebrating since. Joy and freedom are a part of becoming Love, and I think it is time we join the party.

Before we figure out how to have joy while becoming Love, we should think about what joy really is. There are many passages of Scripture that explain that those who know Jesus should have joy in all circumstances.

"Rejoice always, pray without ceasing, give thanks in all circumstances; for this is the will of God in Christ Jesus for you" (1 Thessalonians 5:16–18).

Before my father passed away, this scripture seemed obtainable. Sure! I could be joyful in all circumstances because God is with me in all circumstances. But then the tragedy that changed my trajectory I wrote about in the previous chapter changed everything. How in the world was I supposed to be joyful and rejoice in this darkness? I think we, as humans, will always struggle with distinguishing between rejoicing in the good that Jesus is and feeling the pain of this broken world. We recently sang "Goodness of God" by Bethel Music, and it finally made sense with these lyrics:

> And all my life you have been faithful
> And all my life you have been so, so good
> With every breath that I am able
> *Oh, I will sing of the goodness of God*

The goodness of God are not actions. We see that something is good by seeing what the action and results are. I got a 98 on my test. That is a good grade. I did not get in trouble at school. I have been good. I have been blessed with a great job that I love and that feels good. The good that God is is simply Himself. God is the good. When we sang that all my life God has been faithful, that is not declaring that I have not seen tragedy and felt pain. It is not declaring that those painful moments were the definition of good. *God* was the good in all of my life. We can be surrounded by evil, poverty, death, pain, and war and *still* rejoice because the goodness that exists is God.

But how do we do this? How can we be joyful while trying to be sacrificial love, show mutual love, have equal regard, and embody delivering love?

How do we do this? By being intentional. Go out of your way to make someone feel special. Becoming Love does not have to be only serious. Becoming Love can be about spreading so much joy that it becomes contagious. Let someone show you their favorite comedy and laugh with them for hours. Send a silly text to someone that is having a hard time. As Bob would say, "Live a life of whimsy!" There is enough darkness and brokenness in this world. Let's add to the light!

PART 3
CHANGES EVERYTHING!

Chapter 10

The Gospel (Love Has Come)

> Beloved, let us love one another, for love is from God, and whoever loves has been born of God and knows God. Anyone who does not love does not know God, because God is love. In this the love of God was made manifest among us, that God sent his only Son into the world, so that we might live through him. In this is love, not that we have loved God but that he loved us and sent his Son to be the propitiation for our sins.
> —1 John 4:7–10

Love has been explained in this book by scholars, Jesus, and the memories of my father's actions. We have come to see that Love is much more than a feeling or a cliche or something you say to your family. Love is deep, love is sacrifice, love is forgiving, and love is action. Love has come and that Love is the gospel, *the* good news.

If you happen to have grown up in the south as I have, then you know the word *gospel*. We've got gospel music, gospel services, gospel conferences, gospel books, gospel hymns, and just plain gospel reading. I grew up with this language for the coming of Love and never fully understood how the gospel encompasses the entire Bible to our present and future.

Gospel literally means "good news." You could shout the gospel of Joanna Gaines, which would entail lots of farm style decor and Texas heat. You could shout the gospel of Taylor Swift, which would include love songs, breakup songs, glitter, and friendship bracelets (can you tell I'm writing this during the *Eras* tour?). *The* gospel, the *only* good news that we truly need is that Love has come and Love has a name, Jesus.

My husband and I have recently been attending a new church for us both. We both grew up as staff children in church, and neither one of us ever had to search for what church we wanted because we just went where our parents were. After we got married, we decided we wanted to make that decision in our new family. Except…we have no idea what we were doing. We eventually visited churches after my brother-in-law moved to town and had already done research. We just piggybacked off that research and joined them in their church visit. And we stumbled upon the church we go to now, New City Church.

I could go on about how God has led us to New City. We were welcomed by so many, invited to their small groups called missional communities, prayed over, connected to, and loved on by so many. This was truly a time when I had no mental capacity to reach out, be the one to build relationships, volunteer, and find our spot in the church. I am finishing my second master's degree, working with foster children, and barely seeing my husband and family. But one thing has stood out since we have been going to New City, the gospel.

At New City Church, every Sunday is built around the gospel in four parts: creation, fall, redemption, and restoration. These four words encompass the entirety of the gospel, our purpose, out forgiveness, and our future restoration. The gospel is our connection to God, our redemption from our brokenness, and our hope in our restoration. The gospel *is* love. Only Love would create such an intricate story as a way of being close to us even when we could never be righteous enough. Only Love would take on others' punishment. Only Love would fight for the oppressed. Only Love would see its goodness reflected back from our brokenness. Only Love.

Creation: God created what was adored—light, heaven, night, sky, earth, animals, sea, aquatic life, plants, and humans. This creation was God fully connecting with all of the things He loved. There was no separation, pain, hurt, or division, but God gave humans the ability to choose.

Fall: Under the ability to choose, humans were tempted to make themselves like God. Humans were tempted to look for something better than what God had already given. Humans chose to be separate from the loving Creator, and once humans became unrighteous, God could no longer be in their presence.

Redemption: God created many covenants with humans. God promised to multiply their nations, to never leave them, to love them steadfastly, and to forgive them when they choose temporary happiness over closeness with Him. And humans broke these covenants with God every single time. There was only one way to restore the relationship between the unrighteous human and the righteous God, a scapegoat, in this case, the Lamb of God, Jesus. Jesus is God, so is also Love, as God is Love. Jesus came to show humans how to live a Kingdom-minded life and then gave his own life to fulfill the covenant. Every division, every hurt, and every selfishness was forgiven and removed for those that believed. Humans were redeemed.

Restoration: This part has not come yet. We are still humans that are broken and in need of forgiveness. The world is still broken, lost, and in need of Love to come. The best privilege is those that believe get to be the reflection or glimpse of that Love until we are all made whole in the presence of God.

I have understood the gospel for much of my life, but it took coming to New City Church to find this verbiage of creation, fall, redemption, and restoration. I can look back at my childhood and see where my parents created a life centered on the gospel. My brother and I were loved as the beings we were created to be, and my parents did not ask us or want us to be anything else. We were taught rules and the difference between good and bad and were given consequences when we fell but were forgiven and reminded that nothing we could ever do would cause our parents not to love us. We were taught that we were redeemed through the sacrifice and love of Christ. We were taught to keep this idea close when life was hard or when we messed up. We were taught that through the perfect forgiveness of God, we can be restored with God in His presence.

My father was a counselor before he ever thought about going back to school for counseling. He listened well, made time for others, sought God's teachings with how to defuse conflict, and he loved others well. When I was in middle school, I struggled with my mental health. I did not have the words to explain what it was, but my father understood I was struggling.

I have always been bigger than other girls my age, and as a child, I was made fun of often. I tried to be happy, friendly, and bubbly, and I tried to not let the ugly of the world convince me I was ugly, but I often struggled. One day, I thought about harming myself. I knew I was not going to, but I thought about it enough to get a knife and sit and look at it. My father found out I did this, but he did not scold me or ask what was wrong with me. My father sat with me in my brokenness and repeated how loved I was. He told me how much he and my mother loved me just as I did and that hurting myself was not a good way to deal with my pain. Both my father and my mother gave me cards with their cellphone numbers, work numbers, and Bible verses to remind me they would never leave me and would never stop loving me and that I was loved by God. I kept those cards with me in my wallet for many years knowing I could always count on them.

My parents showed my brother and I what the gospel was and that the gospel truly changes everything. I am just beginning to understand that not every home functioned in this way. I never understood that people had parents that did not listen to them, did not remind them they loved them, and did not do everything they could to keep them safe. I never knew that this was rare.

But it does not have to be.

Love has indeed come, and we should be living like it. The gospel should not just be a concept or something we evangelize about, but it should be our way of life.

Chapter 11

Applying Love

If anyone would be first, he must be last of all and servant of all.
—Mark 9:35 ESV

Application. This was always the moment in school when I really found out what I had learned and if I really learned anything at all. I would call myself a very intentional student growing up. I figured out that I learned better when I wrote things down, so I utilized notecards, handwritten notes in class, copying definitions at home, and writing equations over and over until they stuck. I would find out on test day if my study tactics worked because I would be asked to apply the knowledge I had supposedly learned.

But there was one problem. I often psyched myself out due to anxiety and would miss points that I actually knew. Later in life I would find out that this soul-crushing phenomenon was called test anxiety.

My parents always told me that the grade never mattered. They just wanted to know that I had learned something and had done my best to know and apply the knowledge. You would think this would ease that frustrating test anxiety, but I continued to focus on the grade on the test as the measurement of my intelligence. I do not think that I actually thought I was smart until I graduated undergraduate college with a bachelor's degree in chemistry in only four years from Georgia College and State University when my brother told me I probably could have gone to Georgia Tech, one of the biggest and one of the hardest science and engineering colleges in Georgia. I had made Cs in college. I had cried over failed tests. I had been so confused when I would be able to nearly teach the study sessions with friends but would make the lowest score on the test out of all of us. I did not feel smart because I thought the application of my intelligence solely relied on what I could put on a test. I have come to understand that application is way more about being intentional rather than being correct.

We have trudged through the definitions of love, made the choice to work to become Love, and come to understand more about how Love is the Gospel, but how do we apply it? Is there a test to show that I fully know (or at least know enough for a passing grade) what Love is? Thankfully, there is no test, but what we do have is our lives. Our lives become the evidence of how we have chosen to become Love.

My father's life was an amazing picture of his lifelong attempts at becoming Love. He gave when he had nothing to give. He prayed when he needed to hear God's voice. He listened to the pain of others and held them close as they wept. He taught hundreds of teenagers that they were loved and that someone cared about what they were going through. And he did not wait for an invitation to do anything of this. He learned about Jesus, learned from Jesus, then did his best to imitate how Jesus commanded us to live.

The first way my father applied what it meant to become Love was by taking the time to learn. He made space to learn from other people, he read books, he read the Bible, he sat with people with different perspectives and opinions, and he learned while living a humble life. We can sometimes seek to learn about others from a position of higher than, but as we discussed in chapter 3, mutual Love does not place itself higher than others. My father's genuine interest was in others and understanding their lived experiences better. He never thought he was finished learning because he often sought out people different from him to better apply how he was becoming Love. He continued to be open to learning as long as God was willing to teach him.

The next way my father applied how he was becoming Love was by practice. For all of the wonderful things I have written about my father, he was still a human who made mistakes. He has judged before really understanding someone's perspective, he let the hypocrites and sinful people in the world create some cynicism in his mind; and he had selfish moments. He had to practice applying love to his everyday life to really start to become Love. I remember that he would read the Book of James from the Bible over and over because it mapped out the steps it takes to start to live like Jesus:

> Count it all joy, my brothers, when you meet trials of various kinds, for you know that the testing of your faith produces steadfastness. And let steadfastness have its full effect, that you may be perfect and complete, lacking in nothing. If any of you lacks wisdom, let him ask God, who gives generously to all without reproach, and it will be given him. (James 1:2–6)

Dad had plenty of reason to let the trials of his life interfere with becoming Love. He lost so many things including people, job opportunities, money, health, and time. He could have let those trials build up a wall of bitterness, causing him to not even try to embody Love. But he read the book of James over and over, learning how to use his trials to build his steadfastness and continually asking God for wisdom. He never reached a moment in his life where he decided he knew enough because those that are becoming Love know that they do not know everything.

The last way my father applied how he was becoming Love was by teaching others how to chase Jesus. Dad understood how easy it is to let the pain and suffering of this world take hold of us, especially teenagers searching for their identity. My father spent his life guiding people to live a life of love and light. He desperately wanted the teenagers in his life to not lose hope or focus on becoming Love because Love is our true identity.

Applying the idea of loving others has now been broken down into three realistic steps of learning, practicing, and teaching. The best part about this formula is that Jesus modeled it! Jesus learned about connecting to God the Father. It has always been confusing to me that Jesus is wholly God and wholly human. His humanity did not lessen his divine being but gave us ways to become Love as fallible humans. Jesus as a preteen was found in the temple learning and reading God's word:

> After three days they found him in the temple, sitting among the teachers, listening to them and asking them questions; and all who heard him were amazed at his understanding and his answers. (Luke 2:41–47)

Jesus's father, Joseph, thought Jesus had joined the family in returning to their hometown but later noticed Jesus was not in the caravan of people traveling. They found Jesus in the temple sitting among teachers, listening, and asking questions. How encouraging is it that Jesus sought to understand God more while working to become Love?

Jesus also practiced becoming Love. Now you may not see where I'm going with this because you may be thinking, *Isn't Jesus already Love?* Yes, Jesus is the Love we are becoming, but He used His time on earth to practice becoming Love so that we may see how to do it. Jesus sought people different from Him and His friends. He ate with the town's least popular people, those the religious would label as the greatest sinners, and He listened to the heartbreaking story of a Samaritan woman whom His culture was taught to hate.

> And he had to pass through Samaria. So he came to a town of Samaria called Sychar, near the field that Jacob had given to his son Joseph. Jacob's well was there; so Jesus, wearied as he was from his journey, was sitting beside the well. It was about the sixth hour. A woman from Samaria

came to draw water. Jesus said to her, "Give me a drink." (For his disciples had gone away into the city to buy food.) The Samaritan woman said to him, "How is it that you, a Jew, ask for a drink from me, a woman of Samaria?" (For Jews have no dealings with Samaritans.) Jesus answered her, "If you knew the gift of God, and who it is that is saying to you, 'Give me a drink,' you would have asked him, and he would have given you living water." (John 4:4–10)

Jesus took the path that went straight through Samaria, home of the people group hated by Israelites. Why would Jesus go through a town that He knew could bring disaster? Because he was practicing being Love. He created a situation where He would encounter someone completely different from Him that desperately needed to see true Love. He placed Himself in a vulnerable situation of needing water and being alone in a town of a hated people group all to show Love. Because of this encounter, the woman would testify of all Jesus spoke, which would bring many Samaritans to believe in Jesus as the Son of God. An entire hated people now knew Love!

Jesus also taught others how to become Love. This may be the most obvious way that Jesus applied becoming Love because His teachings and sermons are some of the most widely known and quoted passages of the Bible.

> Seeing the crowds, he went up on the mountain, and when he sat down, his disciples came to him.
>
> And he opened his mouth and taught them, saying:
>
> "Blessed are the poor in spirit, for theirs is the kingdom of heaven.
>
> "Blessed are those who mourn, for they shall be comforted.

"Blessed are the meek, for they shall inherit the earth.

"Blessed are those who hunger and thirst for righteousness, for they shall be satisfied.

"Blessed are the merciful, for they shall receive mercy.

"Blessed are the pure in heart, for they shall see God.

"Blessed are the peacemakers, for they shall be called sons[a] of God.

"Blessed are those who are persecuted for righteousness' sake, for theirs is the kingdom of heaven.

"Blessed are you when others revile you and persecute you and utter all kinds of evil against you falsely on my account. Rejoice and be glad, for your reward is great in heaven, for so they persecuted the prophets who were before you." (Matthew 5:1–12)

Jesus used every opportunity to teach the ways of the Kingdom of God. Jesus wanted his followers to become Kingdom-minded as we discussed earlier in this book. Jesus knew that for people to imitate Him and work to become Love, they would have to be Kingdom-minded. Jesus's teaching flipped humanity's ideals upside down because it focused on putting others first. Jesus knew that this teaching would be difficult, which I think is why He chose to apply Love with action.

Chapter 12

A Changed World

> For the woman that wants to see a change in this
> season: It might have to start with you.
> —Go + Tell Gals

What would a world without war look like? Easy. Heaven. In the broadest and most literal sense of the word. If there were no more wars, greed would not be a factor. Division would not have a home. The oppressed would have freedom. I'm writing this portion in October 2023, during the war in Israel and Gaza and the Hamas terrorist group. I have become overwhelmed with grief and the heavy weight of watching such tragedies unfold. Due to the wide use of social media and technology, we are seeing the real destruction of a people group as a way to destroy the Hamas terrorist group. Hamas are using their own people as shields in this war and have little care for any human life. The Israeli government and military are hoping to wipe their presence off the face of the earth, even if it means destroying the Palestinian people along with Hamas. It's all too much. I can find no right answer. I pray for God to bring peace, freedom to all that are oppressed, including the Jewish people and the Palestinians who are unfortunate enough to be shields of terrorists. I pray for redemption in this world. I pray for the right words and actions because there is little else I can do.

But what did we just discuss in chapter 10? Applying Love. How do we do that when everything is so broken? Applying Love changes the world. But how?

I currently work with foster children. I have come to learn that the foster care system is tragically broken as the rest of the world around us. Families are broken, traumatized, and hurting. I cannot fix the foster care system. I cannot fix the pain I see in the families I work with.

But I can apply Love.

I can be kind to the children that act out and show their aggression as a result of being in the foster care system. I can learn more about therapeutic interventions that can bring relief to such a broken life. I can use my time to think of better ways to relate to those families struggling in this system. I can pray for God to use my words and actions to show Love.

How will any of this fix the wars and pain globally?

It won't.

Unless we all start working to become Love.

I have heard over and over that the world just needs Jesus. While that statement is true, I have never heard of a suggestion of what that looks like. Do we all just stare as the world burns, waiting for Jesus to come again on his white Judgment Day horse? The interesting part about that sentiment is that we can work to become Love ourselves. We can be the only glimpse of Jesus that some may see in their life. We can be the reflection of true and perfect Love. Jesus does indeed change us, but we cannot wait for a grand entrance when God sent us to each other.

Bob Goff once said, "God doesn't just give us promises. He gives us each other." This should be a major invitation for us to act like the gift we are supposed to be for those around us. No matter what is going on in our lives, we can always share a smile, be kind, and listen to others. We can also receive love and help from others because while we were sent to be a gift, we were also sent to be in community. This is reflected in Jesus when he told the disciples to leave Mary alone after she anointed him by cleansing his feet with expensive ointment. Jesus absolutely came to serve and be the ransom for us all, but Jesus also understood that it is a beautiful gesture to allow someone to honor him.

Now do not misunderstand. I do not think sitting around and pretending the world is not on fire and that it will all be fine is what God nor Bob meant. We are ambassadors for Christ!

"Therefore, we are ambassadors for Christ, God making His appeal through us. We implore you on behalf of Christ, be reconciled to God" (2 Corinthians 5:20).

What is an ambassador? Good ole trusty Google can help me out with this one. An ambassador is "a person who acts as a representative or promoter of a specified activity." As people who are "representatives" of Jesus to the world, we must speak against evil, serve those in need, and stand against oppression. God desperately wants people to come to Him and be loved by Him. God appeals His case of His everlasting love to others through us. But how can this happen if we refuse to be Jesus's "representatives"?

Ambassadors are also seen as leaders. When someone is the ambassador for a country, they represent the people of that country and lead and advocate for them. I think this may be the point at which many Jesus followers start to struggle. When those that are becoming Love step into their role of being an ambassador for Christ, they could feel a sense of power and may feel better than unbelievers and maybe other followers. I think this was one of the traits of my father becoming Love that I admired the most. He did so much for so many, led groups of people, spoke to crowds, advocated in the courtroom for teenagers, but if you would have met him on the sidewalk, you would have never guessed all that he did.

One of Dad's former youths told me that my father was the first person to tell her that "oftentimes being a leader means taking a step back and listening or serving." My father had practiced this skill his whole life. He worked hard to pay attention when people spoke to him and genuinely cared about their lives. He would take care of all the small details in his youth ministry as to steward the church's money well and not put extra burdens on others. Being an ambassador for Christ and working to become Love is not a one-way ticket to fame and power. Becoming Love does not end in wealth and abundance. Becoming Love in a world obsessed with power means leading from the back of the line.

What if we do not live into the truth that we are ambassadors for Christ? One of my favorite authors, Jess Connolly, has recently written a book titled *Tired of Being Tired*, and she is speaking and promoting it as I write this. She was quoted saying that many of the "self-help" feelings and ideas were ideas born in the Bible. Jess went on to describe the action of saying self-affirmations to boost self-esteem for those that struggle with loving themselves. But Jess added one caveat, saying that we are strong and enough does not tell the truth that we are who we are because of the goodness of Christ. An affirmation that speaks to this truth could be "I am an ambassador for Christ. I am a child of God." Owning this identity can be the difference in watching the world suffer, hoping Jesus will come back and stepping out and becoming Love as a true ambassador of Christ.

CHAPTER 13

Love in Action Changes Everything

> When you look for the bad, expecting it, you will get it.
> When you know you will find the good, you will get that.
> —Eleanor H. Porter, *Pollyanna*

We have discussed how becoming Love is a life of action. We have seen that love can be shown through sacrificial love, mutual love, equal regard, and delivering love. We have looked at how Jesus embodied these definitions to show us how to become Love. And I have shown you how this can actually work in a regular person's life through the stories of my father.

Our church, New City Church, regularly teaches and ministers the truth, that the gospel changes everything. I felt like this concept, like the concept of creation, fall, redemption, and restoration, was a concept I understood but never had the vocabulary. Once I heard, "The gospel changes everything," out loud, I knew I understood what that meant because I watched those words in action for over half of my life.

Previously, I spoke about how the trajectory of my father's life was changed by the tragedy of his father passing. The miracle that became my father's legacy was Love in action. He would live a life of loving others, seeing them, knowing them, and walking with them, to get to know Jesus even before he was truly trusting in God's path. This realization helps me know that I do not have to know exactly what to do or how to do it flawlessly. I can struggle, change paths, grieve, and still continue to learn how to love in action.

The tragedy of losing my father when I was only twenty-two years old has shaped my life in ways I never would have expected. Before he passed, I saw my father as a great dad, husband, and minister who chose difficult jobs because he wanted to help teenagers. It wasn't until he passed that I really began to fully understand the motivation behind his actions. Now that I am older, I have learned how hard it is to continue to love difficult people in a world telling us to only fend for ourselves. I have seen the pain that oppression and greed has been thrust upon humanity since the day we chose our path and desires over God's desires. Dad changed the world not because he was famous or was a savior; he changed the world by becoming Love. I knew that I wanted God to use me, but it was not until my father passed that I wanted to know what it would be like to follow God so closely that people no longer see me but see Jesus.

My father was not alive during the global pandemic that lasted from 2020 to 2021 and some into 2022. This was a time in our history that has changed the entire world forever. Fear, sickness, pride, selfishness, pain, and darkness covered much of this time. It was very easy to tune out the world and just fend for ourselves. It took stepping back to see how Jesus would have acted to remember that we are working to become Love.

> But woe to you, scribes and Pharisees, hypocrites! For you shut the kingdom of heaven in people's faces. For you neither enter yourselves nor allow those who would enter to go in. Woe to you, scribes and Pharisees, hypocrites! For you travel across sea and land to make a single proselyte, and when he becomes a proselyte, you make him twice as much a child of hell as yourselves.
>
> Woe to you, blind guides, who say, "If anyone swears by the temple, it is nothing, but if anyone swears by the gold of the temple, he is bound by his oath." You blind fools! For which is

greater, the gold or the temple that has made the
gold sacred? (Matthew 23:14–17 ESV)

Jesus spent much of His time trying to get the religious leader to understand that the rules and regulations were not as important as those that needed the salvation and love of God. The global pandemic highlighted our human greed and self-preservation over the care of others. We became overcome with fear rather than working to become Love and figure out how to care for each other. We are all permanently wounded from the pandemic. We were isolated, surrounded by fear and uncertainty, and lost in our own spiraling thoughts. Closing in on ourselves became some of the only ways we could keep our sanity. It became so easy to ignore the pain of others that we are still struggling with reaching out now in 2024. Becoming Love and living out the gospel can truly change everything if we make it a priority over our own preservation. But how do we know that this gospel is the truth and is trustworthy?

Our church recently did a sermon series on the Book of Titus. The passage of chapter 3, verses 8 to 11 was titled "The Gospel is Trustworthy." This passage focused on the importance of trusting Jesus, the True Gospel.

"The saying is trustworthy, and I want you to insist on these things, so that those who have believed in God may be careful to devote themselves to good works. These things are excellent and profitable for people" (Titus 3:8).

Paul was writing to Titus to trust that the gospel is trustworthy and to root out all false gospels that were being presented on the island of Crete, where the church had just begun. We look at biblical stories like this one, and maybe we think, *Well, of course that is a false gospel! How could they not have known!* But do we truly, fully, 100 percent believe in the truth of the gospel? What about when we feel pressured to be a certain type of Christian because it is the "right" way to be a Christian? What about when the world tries to question if God is truly good?

Ouch. That last question got me.

I just described the tragedy of losing my father above. I truly do not see the good that has come out of his death. There was so much good he could have done all these years. So many lives changed because my father could show even more people how to become Love. I may get a glimpse at why God's plan went the way it did, but I do not think I will ever fully understand why my father had to die when he did, at least on this side of heaven.

But that's the problem with limited human thinking. We don't understand what good really is.

I have trusted that good is a healthy baby born at the right time. A home just the right size for a growing family. The right job that seems to fit the passion and financial needs of a family. A beautiful life ending peacefully after many decades of life. A victory over oppression and a deliverance from pain. All of these things seem good, right? We get so caught up in believing in good *circumstances* that we do not look deeper to what God is teaching us—God is good. *Any* goodness in this world is the presence of God. The good in our lives are not the blessings and comfort we have, but the fact that God dwells in us. God is the good! This is how everything changes! When more and more of us work to become Love, it gets easier to see the goodness around us. And seeing this goodness is contagious.

Have you ever heard of an old movie called *Pollyanna*? This was an old movie I watched with my mother when I was young. Pollyanna was a young girl that was full of hope and joy and loved to spread it around. She moved to a very grumpy town and slowly began helping people see the good around them. The best part? When Pollyanna fell from a tree and broke her leg, sending her into a struggle with depression, the whole town showed up at her home to encourage her for all the good she had shown them. Seeing the goodness is contagious! Now what if this goodness and kindness that Pollyanna shared was multiplied by one thousand based on the definition of love we have discussed? What could happen in our world? Becoming Love is not easy, can be a burden, but is one of the best choices we could ever make. Not because it makes our lives better but because Love changes *everything*!

Epilogue

Why Tell David Paul's Story? He Gave Freely of Himself, His Love, His Life

> Tell your story because your story will heal
> you and it will heal someone else
> —Iyanla Vanzant

Why write down what David Paul did? Why did I feel like his story needed to be told? Why did this story in my life have to be told? Because Love does.

This last section may seem very selfish. I am no world-class scholar. I am not a fancy, published author as I write this. I am a daughter that has learned about love not only from seminary but also from watching my father live his life. My father, Reverend David Paul, worked hard his whole life to hear the voice of God and to walk in the direction of Love. I also wanted the world, or at least the bit of the world that may read this, to know that someone like David Paul lived and loved in this world. I want people to know that it can be done. We can truly choose to love without judgment or bias and can indeed follow Jesus's command to serve others.

I want people to know that we do not have to succumb to the hatred or apathy of this world.

Before I talk about my experience growing up with my father, I want to pause with the sentence above. We do not have to succumb to the hatred or apathy of this world. At first, I only wrote hatred, then later I added apathy because I think this tends to seek past us. As followers of Christ, we may find it easy to not hate others. We talk about how Jesus loved all people, and we try not to hate or be judgmental. What we may not think about is when we succumb to our apathy.

According to Google, apathy is the "lack of interest, enthusiasm, or concern." While I do not think we all have to be super enthusiastic about learning to love others, even difficult people, I do think becoming Love has to include having concern for others. We may fall into the trap of apathy when we have been wronged or hurt by others or when we see how dark the world can get with pain and suffering. We may start to believe that it is a waste of time and energy to be interested in others and have a level of concern for the world around us. This idea can be explained by the thought that since as believers we will live eternity with God, we do not have to worry about this earthly world. But God did not call us to lack concern for others. Actually, it is quite the opposite!

"Do not neglect to do good and to share what you have for such sacrifices are pleasing to God" (Hebrews 13:16).

It is pleasing to God to do good to those around us and sacrifice for those in need. This is a call for intentional concern for those around us. God does not want us to be on autopilot. God is pleased when we look around us and see how we can help. Our concern for others is not just a good idea for someone working to become Love but a command from our King.

I never questioned if I was loved growing up. I knew it because my parents told me, showed me, and repeated this daily. I also saw them love others just as fervently. My father knew that many teenagers did not have such love at their homes so he made it his life mission to make sure any teenagers he came in contact with knew they were cared for and loved. These were not the actions of someone playing the savior role or someone that thought they could save everyone in trouble. These were the actions of a man that fervently listened to the voice of Jesus and acted upon Jesus's commands.

As I write this, it has been over ten years since my father passed. I am still processing his death daily. While I may not live life strictly through the filter of his absence as I did the first few years after he passed, I am still learning how his passing is continually impacting my daily life and future. I think this process is one of the main reasons why I felt compelled to share his story. I have learned that my father was not just the "normal" that everyone thinks a father should be. The more people I meet, the more I realize the rarity of people like my father. The important part about sharing his story is trying to share that people like him do not have to be rare. We can all choose this life, but it is not easy.

My father passed away February 7, 2010. The month before, he began to write a book about me. He only got through the introduction before he died. He wrote words about the woman I was becoming and did not even know I would ever become. He wrote about parts of myself that I have only just now begun to understand. He saw so much more in me than I ever saw in myself. I think this small glimpse into how he really thought about me is why I just had to write this book.

Many women get to have their father walk them down the aisle when they get married. Many get to have their parents present at their college graduation. Many get to give their fathers grandchildren. I have not and will not get to experience these things. I did not get to have an adult relationship with my father. When I was having a crisis of faith and career, I did not have him to talk it out. Because of this, I hold this small introduction of his only book so close to my heart. People need to know that there was someone in this world that deeply loved and cared for others. People need to know that love can exist and that we can all be that person.

David Paul was not a perfect person, but he inspired hundreds of people to live a life of love. He inspired me to look deeper at my life and live intentionally. He made no moves to become famous or wealthy. The thing is, he really did not think of himself at all. Hundreds of people came to mourn his absence at his funeral even though he did not start a movement, make millions of dollars, or live a public, lavish life. He loved. Period. It is now our turn. Will we look deeper and live intentionally so that our life is defined by love? Your move.

About the Author

Hannah Rule is an ordained associate licensed professional counselor living in middle Georgia with her husband, Patrick, and is currently a therapist at Lighthouse for Families (a program of the Methodist Children's Home). After hearing her calling from God, Hannah made a career change from a forensic chemist to begin the long journey of vocation discovery. Hannah received her Master of Divinity from McAfee Theological Seminary of Mercer University in 2020, was ordained in 2021, and finally received her master's degree in clinical mental health counseling from Fort Valley State University in 2023. Being inspired by her father's lifelong ministry, cut short at the age of fifty-two in 2010, Hannah begun the work of becoming Love. Hannah invites you to join her in chasing joy and becoming Love at www.hannaherule.com and on Instagram, @herule478 and @lets_dolunch.

Printed in the USA
CPSIA information can be obtained
at www.ICGtesting.com
LVHW042342071224
798390LV00002B/344